SOUL HEALING

Breaking the Chains of Past Life Influence

Reclaim Personal Power Over Addictions,
Dependencies, and Dysfunction.
A Guided Journey to Healing and Wellness

Carole Serene Borgens
and the Divine Spirit Wisdom Source, Pax

Copyright © 2023 Carole Serene Borgens and the Divine Spirit Wisdom Source, Pax.

All rights reserved. No part of this book may be reproduced, stored, or transmitted by any means—whether auditory, graphic, mechanical, or electronic—without written permission of both publisher and author, except in the case of brief excerpts used in critical articles and reviews. Unauthorized reproduction of any part of this work is illegal and is punishable by law.

ISBN-13: 978-1-960583-84-0 print edition
ISBN-13: 978-1-960583-85-7 e-book edition

Published by Waterside Productions
2055 Oxford Ave.
Cardiff, CA 92007
www.waterside.com

High Praise for Pax Spirit Wisdom

Carole Serene Borgens channels the entity known as Pax who thus far, in all the books that have been written, is quite straight-forward. The no-nonsense approach is given to provide tools and actions we must take to heal our selves and our planet. This information is beneficial and very healing if we so chose to follow the guidance. As Pax tells us, it is through our personal power that we will heal. If we begin with our selves in the soul healing process, we shall make great strides to benefit all mankind as well as our planet and beyond.

T. Love, CVST CAPP, EPP
Board Certified Vibrational Energy Therapist

Carole's vast personal knowledge and experience as a nurse, past life coach, automatic writing channeler, and celebrated author, coupled with her 25 years as a pure 'Conduit of Spirt' for Pax, Spokes Entity for Spirit, is a triumph for humanity, and a joyous ride of discovery for all of us seekers! Pax reveals through Carole that there is more to life than this lifetime; there is a vast treasure each of us unfolds as we open to our respective past lives!

This book is a portal, a solid foundation upon which to build an opening to know and embrace our eternal selves, for a planet wide ascension and, as importantly, for us to know our grandness as All One Forever Beings.

Stephen Cipes, Author, *All One Era*

"You, me, and absolutely everyone on this planet has their own self-healing abilities. It is a question of whether yours has switched on or not. This book has the ability to help those seeking the next level to tap into and embody this aspect of themselves, bringing not just the next step of opening to consciousness, but also healing thy self.

Your journey here on this planet is part of a long series of lifetimes. Your only job here now, is to remember who you are and embody your true infinite self. In this understanding, all illness and 'dis-ease' transmutes through the power of you. If you have never heard of such a thing, or dare to believe in it, you have picked up this book for a reason. And there is no doubt this is your time to open to your true understanding of the unlimited possibilities that awaits, on this next step in your journey. Don't think about. Test yourself. If you are unable to set this book down and walk away, r keep thinking about it while trying to decide whether to purchase it, your time has come.

Dive in and plumb to the very depths of why you are here now. It is a beautiful ride! Carole Serene and her ageless wisdom is the next step on your journey. Embrace it now."

Dr. Mandy Simon

Dedication

This writing is dedicated to my fellow travelers: those of you who feel the feelings, the inner stirrings of previously known knowledge, but do not know why. This is for you and your journey.

With guidance from the Divine Wisdom Source and Spirit Messenger called Pax, we are enabled and empowered to understand these inner stirrings, connect with our missing pieces, and find wholeness and healing in this lifetime. This is our purpose and our joy.

And to Pax, whose journey with me has brought blessings and fulfillment of a life purpose I did not see coming, I give my deepest respect, love, and gratitude.

–Carole Serene Borgens

Acknowledgement: Soul Fairies Cover Art

Thanks to my beautiful, talented, and intuitive mother, Lila Borgens, for her gift: the cover illustration for this book, which we title "Soul Fairies."

Although drawn almost 100 years ago, the theme matches that of this book. Seeking what may be, climbing up through hardship, reaching for guidance, recognizing it is there in one's Higher Self, and trusting in the journey to wellness and personal power; this is the message.

Lila must have known I would need this when, as a child, she sketched it with pen and ink in about 1925. This sketch was then sent with an application to a fine-art school, for which she won a scholarship. But lack of finances, and the need to remain working on the family farm, did not permit her to attend.

Despite this disappointment, she remained positive, and her talents continued to blossom. She filled her life with creativity of all kinds. Her hands could make or repair anything and her heart was always happy to share..

My mother Lila's flame burned brightly and brought joy to all through into her 101st year.

Our Healing Philosophy

There can be no healing of Soul pain without understanding the source, the root of the injury and trauma, and this is our journey of exploration with you now. Smoothing out the wrinkles between past lifetimes and present, releasing those deep wrinkles into the ether: this opens new potential for positive growth in the present moment.

Lift up the self by the Self
And don't let the self droop down,
For the Self is the self's only friend
And the self is the Self's only foe.

~from the *Bhag*avad Gita

This Soul Healing journey is a gift to the
you of past, present, and future.

Blessed Wellness

It is our way
It will be yours
Set the intention
Visualize and feel
Believe and trust.

We feel the healing energy within us
We expel the healing energy on our breath for others
Blessed Wellness we hold in our hearts and minds
Blessed Wellness we send as intention to others.

We surround our selves
with the white light of love's protection.

from The Divine Spirit Wisdom Source, Pax.
A reminder that we each have the power to heal.

This book is your invitation to explore the
deeper mysteries of your true nature.

Contents

High Praise for Pax Spirit Wisdom iii
Dedication v
Acknowledgement: Soul Fairies Cover Art vii
Our Healing Philosophy ix
Blessed Wellness xi

Stages of the Soul Healing Journey xv
Your Healing Intention xvii
Introduction xix
Who Really Wrote This Book? xxi
Who is this Spirit and Divine Wisdom Source, Pax? xxiii

Chapter 1: How Did You Get Here? 1

- Your Wounded Inner Child 2
- Accessing Your Higher Self .3
- Reclaiming Personal Power .4

Chapter 2: How Did I Get Here? The Author's Experience 7

- A Shared Purpose 8
- A Personal Journey Inward .9
- A Wounded Warrior 10
- My Curious Lifetime Visited - Too Much Wine and a Goat . . 13
- The Butterfly Emerges - First we learn; then, we teach. 15

Chapter 3: Are You Who You Think You Are, or Should Be?....19

- Finding the Future in Your Past 20
- Returning Balance to Your Life 22
- Are You Living Your Master Plan? 23
- The Joy of Discovery. 24

Chapter 4: Recognizing Spirit Guidance in Your Life 27

- Trust in self and Self 28
- See the Past. 30
- Feel the Past 31
- Believe the Past. 31
- Release the Past. 31
- Emerging into Your Now. 32
- Healing Through Time 33
- Energy Healing and the Mind Body Connection. 33

Chapter 5: The Soul Healing Process 37

- Finding Your Bliss 37
- The Pathway Opens 38
- Transformational Path to Wellness 39
- The First Steps Taken 42
- Lightness of Being – Found 44
- Meeting Your Past: What to Expect 45
- Visualizing the Journey. 46
- Affirmations for Wellness 49

Chapter 6: Recognizing Origins of Current Dis-Ease. 53

- Emotional and Mental Health Challenges 55
- Where Does Hatred Originate? 55
- Where Does Fear Originate? 56

- Where Does Depression Originate? 57
- Where Does Anger Originate? 58
- Where Does Addiction Originate? 59
- Where Does Anxiety Originate? 60
- The Woman's Healing Journey. 62
- The Man's Healing Journey 63
- Recognizing Your Innate Wisdom 63

Chapter 7: Opening a Portal to Your Past: Visualization Techniques 67

- Soul Memory – Your Personal Akashic Records 67
- Opening a Portal to Your Past – Your Higher Self as Guide . . 70
- Opening a Portal to Your Past – Self Guided Visualization. . . 72
- Entering a Portal – The Elevator Method 72
- Talking to Your Past Self – A Healing Conversation 74
- Healing Path Affirmations 77
- More Past Lives, More Present Healing. 77

Chapter 8: Liberation: Living Your New Story 81

- Personal Power Seeds for Wellness 82
- Your Personal Archive of Lives to Access 84
- The Wind Beneath Your Wings 87
- Addictions Understood – Personal Journeys 88
- Alcohol Dependency 88
- Drug Abuse 91
- A Need for Gambling 93
- Co-Dependence: Healing the Broken Spirit 96
- Depression in Men of Today 99
- A Woman's Depression. 102
- A Man's Anxiety 103
- Uncontrollable Anger, Rage 106

- Racism, Intolerance, Superiority 108
- Physical Self-Abuse. 111
- Gifted or Mentally Ill? 114
- Healing Residual Past Life Guilt: Another Visit Needed?. . .116
- The Personal Pace of Healing 118
- Are You Among the Wisdom Keepers? 119
- Reclaiming Personal Power. 121

Chapter 9: Soul Healing for Weight Management 125

- Releasing The Chain 125
- A Transformational Path to Wellness – What to Expect . . . 126
- Viewing the Past: Stories Told and Healing Found. 130
- From Cold Confinement to Chronic Overeating. 130
- Long-Term Diet to Long-Term Binge: She Thought She Was in Control. 132
- Historical Food Stealing and Hoarding – Finding Her Link to Over-Eating Now 134
- Royalty and Body Image – The Binge-Purge Cycle. 135
- Anorexia, Bulimia, and Food-Body Relationships through Time 136
- His Lifetime Food Dependency: Soul Healing Led Him to Self-Mastery 138
- The Thread of Life Contained in Soul Memory 140
- Will You Choose a High Road or Low Road? 140
- Who Speaks Loudest, Your Heart or Your Head? 142

Chapter 10: Soul Healing: Accessing Your Inner Guidance . . . 145

- Entering the Portal: Your Journey to Past Lifetimes Begins. . .147
- Meeting Your Past Self – A Presence in Both Worlds. 150
- The Expanded Four-Stage Process 153

Chapter 11: After the Epiphany 161

- A Personal Reflection: Healing the Crack in Her Soul 161
- Living the Empowered You. 164
- Gifted Old Souls Need Healing Too 165
- Stepping Into Your Truth. 166
- Is Soul Healing About Karma?. 167
- Will You Share Your Light with the World? 168
- Personal Power for Earth Healing 168
- A Gift Received Is a Gift to Be Given – Personal Power for Earth Healing 169

Stages of the Soul Healing Journey

Inspiration
Peace, healing, harmony, wellness, and joy. For all people to experience these feelings and ways of being in their daily lives, this is the inspiration within this book.

Vision
Imagine the personal power that would be reclaimed if everyone entered the gates to their past lives and history, saw what was there for them, and benefited from it in today's life.

Power
Our personal history is available to all who are inspired to enter these gates. We show the way for all to visit past lives, recognize ongoing challenges, and release what no longer serves.

Purpose
Find your truth in history, so you may thrive today. We inspire hope in those seeking direction to their wellness and freedom, so they may emerge as the butterfly and soar into their grand celebrations of present life, wellness, and joy.

Transformation
Follow your guided Journey to Wellness and freedom from the bonds of addictions, dependencies, and dysfunction. Release what was and move into your full potential.

Living the Empowered You

Your world, your way. Joy, peace, harmony – all yours to claim in this lifetime. With personal power restored, you can shine the light for others on their Paths to Wellness.

Your Healing Intention

We each have experienced physical or emotional wounds (trauma) in past lifetimes, and those unresolved hurts are imprinted on our Souls. It is our Souls that travel with us through lifetimes, and if we can identify and heal those past hurts, we clear our present life from associated limitations and challenges. There can be no healing of Soul pain without understanding the source, the root of the injury and trauma. This is our journey with you now.

It is possible to heal current life challenges by healing connected past life traumas. Understanding that you are not the creator of today's challenges but do have the power to make change is liberating. Truly separating your present life from your past allows for transformation.

We also bring talents, gifts, and great abilities forward from past lives, whether academic, artistic, or athletic. As an example, "child prodigies" have been recognized for centuries and the source of their gifts goes unquestioned.

For the purpose of this writing, however, our focus will be on challenges faced by many in this present lifetime that can be linked to past incarnations and trauma experienced in those times. Our journey is to heal current challenges and dis-ease by healing past life trauma.

In this writing is our wish for all people to have access to this self-healing process. How to accomplish this, when we are one and those wanting to gain this knowledge are many? Taking that question to Pax resulted in this book, the purpose of which is to present the method for each person to identify their source of current life challenges; connect them to pertinent past lifetimes; and begin the healing process – all while wrapped in the protective love of Spirit.

"A Healing Journey of any kind can be an adventure. Some like to go alone, while others prefer travel with a guide. This Soul Healing process is aided by your Inner Guidance.

Know that you journey with your Higher Self as guide, protector, and greater wisdom while entering onto this, your healing path, is wrapped in love and trust.

Observing your past lives and identifying those impacting your life today begins the healing of your present – this is our gift to you now."

Our intention is to illuminate this path to resolution, to healing, and to releasing these chains of past life influence, in love and caring now for your reclaimed wellness.
~Pax

Introduction
What if None of This is Your Fault?

Have you considered that fears, anxiety, food dependence or avoidance, addictions, depression, anger, or unexplained negative behaviors may not be your fault, and may not be your choice?

What if:
Your compulsive behaviors are directly linked to past lifetimes' conditioning and not the fault of who you are today?

What if:
It is your Inner Child with wounds originating in this lifetime (but linked to the past) that is blocking your attempts to live in peace, wellness, and joy?

What if:
Through this process of healing your Soul (that which travels with you through lifetimes holding the highs and lows of past experience) you can be freed from current triggers and claim your full potential of personal power and happiness? Imagine!.

If each of us has lived past lifetimes, some more than others, it could be true that our star trajectory is influenced by one specific lifetime: that we call the "pivot point" or "pivotal lifetime."

- **What if:**
    We could know that lifetime and what transpired there that left our Soul with scarring that affects our current life choices?

- **What if:**
    We could identify the scarring that remains on our Soul today; heal those old wounds; and release the people involved as well as our selves? What difference would this make to our present wellbeing?

Understanding that you are not the creator of your life challenges but do have the power to change them: this is liberating and empowering. Truly separating your present life from your past lives is transformational beyond words.

There is no end to the amount of personal power one can reclaim. It is about trust, always, and that trust is found within the self and supported by the Higher Self. One need look no further when undertaking this healing journey.

Who Really Wrote This Book?

Soul Healing, the process, is a combination of Universal Wisdom as well as present day strategies and tools for your Journey to Wellness.

This writing is a collaboration, a combination of channeled guidance from the Divine Spirit Wisdom Source, Pax, and personal insight from my self as channel and author.

The writing style alternates throughout the text of this book, moving between my style of writing and speaking to that of Pax, who enters my thoughts when he wishes to speak and add to what I have written. Often, when writing, I begin to feel a sense of free-flowing information and know Pax has joined me to contribute. Ours is always a joyful collaboration!

I leave it to you, the reader, to distinguish between these two writing styles and, therefore, the source. One clue is that Pax speaks in a somewhat formal and almost "old world" manner. This way of speaking appears across all of our published books, and you will come to recognize it as we move between our two voices.

Included in the text are sections of channeled wisdom from Pax not written and presented by me, but rather through me. This channeled wisdom stands apart from my own words, as it is pure wisdom and guidance from Spirit. I am blessed to bring it forward and into this book for all to access.

While I have come to refer to Pax as "he," this Spirit Wisdom Source is not an individual but rather a Universal consciousness. "He" is my convenient term of reference, developed over many years of writing together.

Common throughout all of our books is the underlying intention for all people to find peace and love in their lives, to ensure that personal power remains intact.

Showing the path to healing and reclaiming inner strengths, if diminished, and giving guidance always with love and respect – this is the common theme throughout Pax Spirit Wisdom writings.

Throughout this book are references to "self" and to "Self"; these two terms are very different. The term "self" refers to your daily self, your present day and ego-driven persona. References to "Self" refer to your Higher Self, the all-knowing Inner Wisdom of your Soul, that which has traveled with you through all lifetimes and now guides you in love and protection, if you will allow.

Enjoy!

Who is this Spirit and Divine Wisdom Source, Pax?

The word Pax means "peace" and expands to "Messenger of Peace." The name is appropriate for a Spirit with the intention to contribute peace and love to humanity and Planet Mother Earth.

When I ask Pax about his nature, with the words "who are you," he responds by saying:

"We are one with the Universe, not the Universe alone. We are the Divine Universe, yes, and the greater wisdom, that which knows and supports all and is healing, non-judgmental, and tolerant; all-seeing, all-knowing, and peace."

What does Pax look like?
Over time, there has also been curiosity about the appearance of Pax. Does he look like we might expect? How do we expect a Spirit Wisdom Source and Messenger of Peace to look?

Asking this human-curiosity question of Pax provoked this self-description:

"We are a puff of cloud, a breath of wind, a library filled with knowledge, a raging river, and a vast ocean. We are the circumference of your globe and the weight of it. We are the sound of the jungle and the quiet of snow, while all the while being like the figure Atlas, holding the weight of the world on his shoulder while attempting to support humankind. This is our who and our why and our reason for being with you as a constant."

And now we know.

Allow your self to soar by receiving this wind beneath your wings.

—Pax

01

How Did You Get Here?

Knowing we can choose our parents, choose to blueprint our life trajectories prior to entering this world — would you make the same choices again? This is a question that will be answered in time, and that time is the journey to learn what was and led up to what is, presently. This is a profound revelation, and it brings validation of what you have chosen for this life and, possibly, a surprise or two about why you made certain choices.

It is gratifying to have clarity going forward in life, and so often that comes from having clarity about the past. It was not always you who made choices for your self in past times. So, when those choices and the results of them impact your present wellness, it is worth learning how they can be diffused and released.

The link between past lifetimes and current life experiences is powerful and can be the basis for strain and strife in family relationships today. That you have traveled through time with the same people very often, and always those of your choosing, this can explain a family dynamic where negativity is prevalent. The opposite holds true: the past can positively influence family relationships that have an abundance of love and caring within them.

Your Wounded Inner Child

We address those of you, now adults, who have been subjected to present day childhood trauma to varying degrees. Those internalized memories color your life actions and reactions. This wounded inner you, your Inner Child, has no knowledge of the reasons for your childhood mistreatment or what you may have done wrong. Chances are, there was no wrong-doing, only punishment. Does this feel familiar to you?

Know that the blueprint for life involves each person selecting their life path, including the parents and friends who will accompany us on our journey. Often, the cast of characters is selected for the purposes of healing, continuing deep love, returning kindness, or resolving differences. There are those who direct life's course according to negative reasons, who take negative actions based on their own injured feelings and past experiences. Such decisions bring pain and punishment to relationships, where there should be innocence and love.

The Soul Healing process can extend to the present Inner Child in need of understanding and recognition, also resolution, thereby allowing for release of undeserved and misunderstood feelings of unworthiness and guilt. It is a gift to your self, this process.

As the steps to accessing your Higher Self and your past lifetimes are laid out, the journey can also be guided to hidden memories of this current life. These repressed memories of childhood trauma are still with you, deep down and awaiting discovery and healing. The Soul Healing process can return us to past lifetimes or to present life childhood trauma, each hidden in the deep recesses of the conscious mind.

Past life experiences hidden from present consciousness or current life experiences hidden from the conscious mind: both can be accessed, resolved, and released.

Accessing Your Higher Self

What if we could visit that pivotal time to understand what took place there and has been with us, at least the effects of it have been with us, ever since? Could we forgive who and what we see there and release the connection from then to now? How would we do this?

Let us approach these questions from the viewpoint of a spiritual being having a human experience, as so many in this world are. Soul Healing is designed to be inclusive, and this book wraps its pages of understanding around all readers who can find their selves between these lines.

Each person has a Higher Self they can call upon, one that holds Soul Memories from each lifetime lived. Each person has the ability to make change along their life chain. Is this surprising? It is the domain of each person to determine what they will and will not allow into each lifetime, to determine what will affect their present and future: both of which are within their control. This is a foreign thought for many, but we assure you it is within the realm of not only possibility, but probability that each person can reach back into their hazy past life experiences and pull up the one they wish had not happened.

We say that all experiences are valuable in our formation of Soul reality, but not all are required to remain in inventory. Future wellness can be impacted positively by moving a damaged link in the life chain to the bin reserved for that which no longer serves us.

What is offered to you here and now is a step-by-step guide to healing past or current life trauma and reclaiming trust in your personal power. We share this gift with you and extend blessings for your Journey to Wellness.

This is your invitation to explore the deeper mysteries of your true nature.

Reclaiming Personal Power

As Pax guides us to and through our challenges, we are also guided to the joy of reclaiming our personal power and, as a result, a renewed focus on personal passions.

While we consider our potential for healing, we also must consider that we are here in this lifetime to grow, to flourish, and to bring love and positivity to our selves and our world. Humanity is in great need now of bright light. As we rise from any darkness previously experienced, we shine our light on those around us as well as our forests and animals, air, and soil. With awareness of the dire state of our Planet Earth enveloping us, it is clear we are supported in our journey by our inner Spirit and can make a positive improvement in our world. We are often reminded by Pax of the state of our Planet Mother Earth and our need for conservation.

Do we understand there is a movement toward peace and love on Planet Earth? Do we understand we are part of the healing asked for by our rivers and streams? They call upon us to be the light, to shine our light into dark corners and illuminate the way forward into healing. In this need, we may find our own strengths, our own call to action. It is a global need now: soulful attention to wellness for all people and for Earth's resources.

Past life experiences hidden from present consciousness or current life experiences hidden from the conscious mind: both can be accessed, resolved, and released.

It is only when you stand in your own light that you can illuminate the path for others.

02

How Did I Get Here? The Author's Experience

Coming into this life as an "Old Soul," a Spiritual Being having a human experience, I was drawn to enter a healing profession, so early on became a nurse. Meanwhile, I continued to study psychology, then parapsychology, and was drawn to the study of past lifetimes and regression techniques. It became clear that I was blessed with the gifts of Intuition, Empathy, Mediumship, Channeling, Animal Communication, and what I refer to as Knowingness or Clairsentience. It became clear that I was drawn to helping others find healing in their lives.

My introduction to the Spirit Messenger Pax came in the mid-1990s. It was an evening when I was at my desk at home, receiving Spirit messages via automatic writing. A normal evening for me: all was quiet, my three Irish Wolfhounds lay peacefully sleeping on the carpet, and I was communicating with Spirit.

This normal evening took an unexpected turn when Pax came through in my writing for the first time, with a very different type of energy than I had previously experienced. I received an introduction to him and Pax Wisdom. The energy feeling in my hand and arm changed. The style of writing changed too. What followed was a request that I consider becoming a Pax channel for future messages and writings. It was stated that there was great concern about what was transpiring on Planet Earth, particularly with the environment, and so Spirit wished to speak, to share Universal Wisdom and Guidance for our benefit. That was my introduction to knowing that when Pax speaks, there would be wisdom for the world, and I should listen.

Recognition of the importance of this contact, and request, was immediate. My shocked reaction had me on my feet with the intent of pacing the office floor to think about it all. However, wall-to-wall sleeping Irish Wolfhounds made that impossible. So, I returned to my chair and sat in wonder to contemplate this unexpected and inspiring experience.

Feeling the responsibility attached to this invitation from Pax, I took time to consider it. Over the course of a week or so, I thought long and hard about the question – and ultimately accepted. My agreement with Pax included expectations that I respect his messages; that I not change any of the words; and that I compile the Spirit guidance into book form, so that it could be shared with the world. This became my philosophy and practice.

A Shared Purpose

Since that time, we have published numerous books based on channeled Pax Wisdom. Now my life purpose, my mission is to continue sharing Pax Wisdom with the intention of helping humankind find ways to function in love and wellness on and for our Planet Mother Earth – as individuals recognizing their personal power to make change.

In addition to book writing, we have continued to work closely with people looking for clarity on how their past lifetimes affect them today. We have shared the joy of helping others identify and release triggers to past life events linked to current day dis-ease.

Some of these challenges are addiction, anxiety, anger, fear, PTSD, depression, compulsive behavior, and forms of dis-ease that are physical, psychological, or emotional in nature. All these issues can be linked to past life trauma.

Formal training in techniques of Past Life Regression has been pivotal and the basis for my journey into this realm. Exploring many past lifetimes with people seeking to know their history brought me to the place where I believed there were therapeutic uses for this process, far beyond simply satisfying curiosity. The next step to helping others, then, was to visit and understand my own past lifetimes, where loss of some personal control had originated. So began the journey that resulted in the fullness of the Soul Healing process outlined in this book.

Now I cannot imagine life without this gift of channeling Spirit, or without the daily blessing of collaborating with the Divine Spirit Pax, who shares wisdom and guidance for the benefit of all.

That is my great gift in this lifetime. But we, Pax and my self, have traveled the road together prior to this collaboration, having written (or, rather, channeled) numerous books on a variety of topics.

We have journeyed together in my past lifetimes and have formed a strong bond, being connected by what I view as an invisible but powerfully felt golden cord of communication, protection, joy, respect, and love.

Through investigating my own past lifetimes, I better understand my connection with Pax. Also, I now understand how my blueprint for life has brought me to this point. Years and years of feeling as a square peg not fitting into the round holes of "normal" life, in this Earth School, should have alerted me to what was to come. It has all become clear and revealed. There had been a reason for everything. As there always is.

A Personal Journey Inward

The more personal past lives I visited, the more questions were answered about why I was who I was; why I created the scenarios that characterized my life; and what prompted my pull toward or push away from expectations placed upon me in early life. I came to understand what created my questioning nature about some "solid" family values; why I differed from my parents in philosophy, even as a child; and the source of my bases for thinking or acting. What was the history behind me that I unknowingly carried forward?

Children come into their lives with Soul Memories of who and what they were made of in past lives. I certainly did. Knowing things, feeling energy, having opinions, holding likes and dislikes, and rejecting or accepting what parents and family believe – all this can be a rocky road for children with strong Soul Memory, or Cell Memory, and particularly for those who are Old Souls.

It is said that life is a mystery. It certainly can be, and it can also be explained and understood by knowing a little history (personal past history, that is to say). I can assure you that as the many layers are peeled away and more is revealed of who you once were, the impact on who you are now begins to be felt. There is a shift in your life trajectory. This new awareness is the difference between light and darkness on your life path forward into wellness.

Trust in this. Know that the revelations to come will illuminate your path to personal wellness. It is this faith in your self – to take the first step in what will be many on your personal quest for answers about your history and to regain your inner strengths – that results in the next steps becoming easier, leading to your desired outcome of personal peace and wellness.

Your journey flows with joy and promise for
the healing ahead. It is yours to claim.

A Wounded Warrior

The time was right. I needed to find out who I had been in past lives, particularly those that held me back. So, into the adventure I went. Through past life regression and meeting my past personas, those former selves whose hurts and traumas have connected with me in this lifetime, came the gift that has allowed for my personal healing and wellness today.

With the guidance of Pax on my journey into past lives, there was an incredible flow of energy and the witnessing of numerous brief periods of lifetimes. In some cases, food and alcohol were a focus; in others, they were present recreationally but not in a troublesome way. Deeper investigation was transformative in my gaining of understanding over connections to present life challenges as well as curiosities. It was an inspirational journey into each lifetime, and the lessons learned were instrumental in my release of triggers and moving through to healing.

A memorable visit had me settling into an earlier life as a soldier. Examining present day connections brought a feeling of familiarity. It had been a time of battle for him, that much was clear. But his particular war and time period were not revealed. While this soldier survived and returned home, he was damaged beyond repair in terms of psychological and emotional trauma. How did he cope with this after returning to civilian life, where a normal appearance belied his inner turmoil? Alcohol particularly, and food to a lesser degree, became his crutches and his daily companions in excess. They numbed his conscious reality and offered fleeting periods of shallow peace. Today, similar versions of his story are known as post-traumatic stress disorder, or PTSD. But in his time, that condition was not recognized or understood. It was called by other names, and treatments were often as damaging as the symptoms themselves.

One could say recognition overcame me. More accurately, it built up from within. Finding his historical predicament pertinent to my present life existence, my Spirit reached out to the wounded soldier. We began a dialog, which took me into his heart and mind and allowed me to understand the emotions he felt and how the experiences of war had left him compromised in so many ways. He was unable to cope with the expectations of civilian life. His daily companion, alcohol, numbed his sensitivities and brought him a measure of comfort. It was the only comfort he found in his life back at home, where nothing felt the same as it had been before he left for war.

Through witnessing my Soul experiences during this soldier's lifetime, and comparing with spin-off likenesses in my present life, I saw similarities that answered important questions for me. Cause and effect became clear for the first time, regarding the role of food and alcohol in my life. It was an epiphany, an awakening, a realization that gave me an ability to understand and release the influence of that past time. Nothing in my current life was a cause; it was that past life experience that had created my present life triggers. This freedom from blame was an important part of the lessons to be learned.

I understood, for the first time, why from an early age alcohol felt comfortable to me, familiar even. I seemed to be missing an "off switch," which other people had: the wisdom to recognize that one or two drinks were sufficient. There was an unexplainable familiarity and comfort in the taste and feeling alcohol brought, therefore more would be better (so I thought). More is what my physical body wanted, so more became the norm. It seemed as though my body and mind were missing something, when in reality my body and mind had an extra something. That extra bit was the physical feeling that alcohol was a comfort and good. Intellect was never permitted to enter into decision making; that was bypassed by the body's desire for more that originated with the first taste. There was detachment where there should have been recognition, and denial where there should have been awareness.

What was present in place of that missing off-switch was what I termed a "magnet" for attracting more. The result was a combination of knowing alcohol's effects were being felt and a magnetic pull at a cellular level to take in more, despite this awareness. It became a push-me-pull-me scenario, with the goal being to override conscious awareness of the need to stop. Was this my goal? If so, why? Self-sabotage is the answer, and I knew it but chose to ignore.

This tendency to ignore my own best interests applied also to food at times. How could an otherwise intelligent and nutrition-conscious person, such as my self, consume unhealthy foods, and consume them to excess while knowing the damage they could and would cause? Again, the feeling of familiarity and comfort food provided overtook sensibility and the more-is-better feeling prevailed. The term "comfort food" comes from a deep, emotional place where a void needs to be filled and a lacking exists that will only be satisfied with the fullness of tasting and chewing favorite foods.

I knew that a dialog needed to take place between my self and my former persona: that wounded soldier. Through entering this conversation and helping him recognize and release his demons, there was healing on both sides. My understanding of how and why food and alcohol became a dependency in his life diffused their magnetic pull in mine.

What became apparent to me was the ease of conversation with this past persona of mine, the sense of familiarity and comfort in communicating. We seemed to share a mutual feeling of respect and intention for healing. Sharing with him what we know today of PTSD, and the attached symptoms, brought a release of anxiety and new ability for him to view his situation in a detached and more clinical manner. His feelings of unworthiness were lessened, and he viewed his situation differently. We seemed to meld into an understanding of each other. My visits with him multiplied, and I was able to release the hold of that lifetime and set of experiences. With love and acceptance for his journey, I moved on in my current life with new recognition of the role of alcohol and comfort food as well as diminished appetite for both.

My Curious Lifetime Visited - Too Much Wine and a Goat

As I viewed the scenes of my past lifetimes, some were selected for closer inspection based on their intensity of trauma, or in some cases for their curiosity.

One memorable scene showed a large and open space in what appeared to be early Roman times, or possibly Greek. In this palatial courtyard setting, the remnants of an opulent and lengthy feast were apparent. Left over from the orgy of food and drink were sleeping bodies scattered about. One person, who remained awake and still drinking appeared to be my own self of that time. The only companion, also awake, was a goat. When I asked who was present here, who was left to speak with, I was told "jus' me and the goat" in rather slurred words.

The humor of this scene has stayed with me. While the excess of food and wine was obvious to me, it seemed normal for that place and time in history. My past persona was a guest at the feast who seemed an innocent victim of his own enthusiasm as a novice partygoer. I did not delve deeper into this lifetime, because my feeling was that happiness and wellness prevailed there, and that I had dropped into an unusual, for him, circumstance.

How powerful are these Soul memories that they remain a constant? We must understand ways to find recognition but disallow the past's potential for control in subsequent life patterns – this is found in the Soul Healing process. The ability to diffuse negative influence from my past onto my present life: this was a gift.

Following these and other experiences, I gained a sense of relief from previous excesses that had been part of my present lifetime. Once understood, they seemed to have no further power over me. The behavioral change was supported by an understanding I could not explain – it just was. There came a release of cravings, a release of thinking about alcohol and comfort food, and a release of focus on those previously felt needs. As well, there was release of blame formerly directed inward, now known to originate with past selves that I knew so little about. Now there was recognition and understanding, forgiveness and release of guilt – all of which contributed to my transformation on this Path to Wellness.

The Butterfly Emerges -
First we learn; then, we teach.

The next stage in this healing journey of mine helped me develop gratitude for the awareness of all that led to my understanding, my release of what was, and my transition into present day wellness. Life goes on now with an outward view and an eye toward sharing this process with others in the joy of discovery. Gaining a deep understanding of self and Self brings greater personal power and renewed vision of what is right and acceptable for each person going forward in their life. There began my further study of what was, as it relates to what is. I learned to ask: what are the current life challenges that can be directly traced to unresolved episodes or patterns in past lifetimes? To me, it became logical and quite natural to believe there is a link, a strong causal connection: that people face challenges or limits that stem from non-current life experiences. These show themselves as irrational or unexplained present day behaviors and dis-ease.

The more I investigated, the more reasonable and clear this truth appeared to be. So, I began to formulate a system by which we can regress through past lifetimes to identify trauma or unresolved hurt, both physical and emotional, and so create personal healing. This process was directed to follow links to present life challenges, trigger responses, and unexplained or troublesome negative behaviors. On this journey, there is no need to reexperience a previous lifetime's pain; the subject acts as an observer only. They feel both detachment and protection, which enable continued exploration in comfort and safety.

By observing our past lives, we can also identify strengths, gifts, and talents that have been brought forward to the present day. Understanding these positive inheritances can be just as powerful as recognizing challenges of the past that have negatively affected experiences in our current lifetimes. There are many people whose talents go beyond our understanding, particularly at early ages, and those abilities can be linked to who they were during another period in history. This is a fascinating aspect of past life exploration that leads to greater awareness of the present day self's talents, abilities, and strengths in all ways.

Is it broadly accepted that a "child prodigy" is gifted and exceptional. Do we question how they came to be? Whether appearing in childhood or later in life, exceptional talents largely go unquestioned. The person we say, all-too simply, is "gifted." Similarly, we do not search for answers to why individuals come into this life with negative characteristics and destructive behaviors. Just like remarkable talents, these stem from latent past experiences, which later rise to the surface. We must ask about the source of problems, which plague even those of us who come from healthy family environments.

Whether positive or negative, the residual effect of past life experience will show themselves eventually. If we can understand how to approach diffusing the negatives, they can ultimately be replaced with new beginnings. We can become as positive and powerful as those beings we refer to as gifted.

There is more to this life than this life.

—Pax

03

Are You Who You Think You Are, or Should Be?

When did you first become aware that you have lived past lifetimes? Have you felt that any of them were affecting you in this current life incarnation? Perhaps you are just now beginning to consider that such connections may be part of your story.

It is what we speak of with you now: this unknown, this tugging at your thinking that something that is does not come from you, the today you, the one blamed for wrongdoing as well as acclaimed for successes. We suggest this unknown may be merely triggered by today, activating deep-seated Soul Memory from lives past.

Have you considered that depression, fears, addictions, anger, or unexplained destructive behaviors may not be your fault, and may not be your choice?

If you are thinking this, you are not wrong. We speak now of ways to heal the wounds of those past times, to recognize and understand the trauma you experienced, and to lead you through a process of understanding and release of these Soul Memories and their influence on you.

This is the key to freedom from what has been dormant within you and coloring your actions and reactions for lifetimes. Now it is time to know this and walk away from those past influences, toward peace in your heart and soul.

It has been my privilege to share this process one-on-one with people over the years and guide them through their healing journey of past life recognition and soul clearing. Now I want to share more widely, through this writing, to ensure all people have access to this Soul Healing method as given to me by the Divine Spirit Wisdom Source, Pax.

To each of you, I say trust that you have personal power to make the changes you desire. You are supported by your Higher Self on this, your Journey to Wellness.

Finding the Future in Your Past

In the beginning of your Soul Journey, you may encounter experiences or entire lives of hardship, pain, and all manner of deprivation and inhumanity. That is an almost-inevitable part of returning to the times when civilization was not-so civil. Women and children were treated as chattels, and far-less than equal to men – and servitude brought with it diminished ability to thrive.

Men were expected to be warriors and hunters or were slaves to those possessing wealth and status. Or perhaps it was you who was once wealthy, knowing few hardships. Life found ways of equalizing the haves and have-nots over time, and what we consider here are those on both sides in this inequality of being. The largest or the smallest hurt, or injustice, can live in Soul Memory and become an impossible-to-overlook trigger source.

> *We do not have a soul; we are a soul.*
> *We have a body.*

To gain clarity on exactly what is Soul Memory, we need to understand that previous lifetimes are imprinted on our Soul. What transpired there and then is like a recording that we do not see but know it's there.

This record can be retrieved at will. The signature of those past lifetimes remains with us, unseen and unheard until we decide to release the story.

This is our gift now: to access our story, our past, in order to understand what is needed to heal our present and, by extension, our future. It is not "rocket science," as is said, but is just as powerful.

To recognize a specific trauma in a specific lifetime, to not re-live the pain of that situation but rather observe it: this brings understanding of who, what, when, where, and why, allowing us to release the hold the past has on us and diffuse present day triggers to inappropriate responses. This is the gift – clarity of vision moving forward – your gift.

Pax tells us often that we need to "look to our past to find our future." This applies in so many ways, and this is one. When we know where we came from and what makes us do what we do, particularly when we have not previously understood why, we are gifted with the opportunity to heal and release past behaviors, thereby healing our present. It often takes time to accept and fully adjust, but there is no diminishing the relief experienced through this healing. It is a reclaiming of your own personal power, which has been diluted over time and now returns to fullness.

It is more than healing that comes with understanding our past life personas. Talents and strengths, gifts, and abilities: so many positives may be found through this journey. To recognize the truth and open to what you may have felt stirring within you, but never investigated, this is another journey within to find the joy of deeply rooted abilities. We have spoken of recurrent feelings of being drawn to areas in this life without knowing why. This is where the seeker may find what filled their hearts with joy in a past life, joys that they are destined to repeat and fulfill in the present. It is Soul Memory that has us predisposed to succeed at certain talents, and it is that Soul Memory that will support deeper investigation toward developing what has remained hidden. The time, which is to say your time, has come.

You may have lived as a cherished ruler, and you may have lived as a wise leader. Despite their lofty positions in society, even these souls experienced negativity in their lifetimes, which may continue to impact current lives. Whether lived as king, queen, or chattel, each life had its challenges, much like today.

Returning Balance to Your Life

While we ask that you consider the steps toward wellness as profound, we also ask that you consider your self open and ready to undertake this journey to wellness. Will you? It is clear that the time is now, and the goal is in sight. What is the goal, you may ask?

We see the goal as a return to balance in your life. Balance in optimal physical and emotional health – this is the intention as we move ahead in your Journey to Wellness. Yes, we say journey, because for each person there are steps to be taken to find and then follow their own pathway to the purpose they came into this life to fulfill. For many, this purpose has not been identified, and that is normal. How many people do you know who speak of their life purpose, who even know that their life has a purpose previously established and agreed to between their selves and their Souls? Who knows that they are guided toward fulfillment if they will open to receiving? Indeed, this is the reality. Too often, that path is not followed, making for a rocky road in life.

Believing this and trusting that Spirit (or what you may call the Universe or your Higher Self) has a master plan for you will reveal the blueprint for your journey and the roadmap to follow. Would not such revelations become an asset to you in this lifetime? Will you welcome the idea of allowing this gift into your consciousness and taking guidance from within? When you open to the wisdom contained within you, within your Higher Self, that which has traveled with you through all lifetimes, there is nothing you cannot manage. You become empowered with this base of knowledge and have clarity going forward: clarity and your personal army of ancestral Guides ensuring your path is clear.

Are You Living Your Master Plan?

Here we are at the beginning, the place where we jump in or jump off. Trusting in your self, now, to forge ahead into the exploration of what your Higher Self has to share with you: this is the adventure. Knowing this is what you have agreed to, for this lifetime healing should bring confidence. We say "should," because each person can use a boost of confidence from time to time. Do you know that you do not walk alone on this path? That you are powerfully supported?

As you undertake this Soul Healing process, know that you may be alone in a room, but you are not alone on this journey; your Guides are with you. This experience is to be undertaken in open-hearted joy at the prospect of communication with your protective Spirits and with your Higher Self. We extend this gift to you in love; it is a first step to healing.

Have you often felt inner strengths, ones you could not imagine the source of? Have you wondered how you developed them? This is an exciting question for you to build upon, not to deny. Each person, while they may have fears and weaknesses, also has strength and talent. It is each person's responsibility to focus on healing as well as growing their positive inner traits. When we recognize what is and why it is so, we are empowered to separate our strengths from our challenges and approach each in the best possible way.

Obstacles along the way will be presented, certainly. They will often come in the form of family and friends who fear for your wellbeing and consider you perfectly fine as you are, who feel that there are no reasons to look so deeply within your Spirit for answers. This can be denial, due to fear, although concern is often expressed in the name of caring.

We are here to bring balance back into lives, and the journey being undertaken is one followed with eyes and heart wide open. The trust of each person in their selves is key and trusting in our Higher Selves even more so. Our intention is to propel each person to know their higher purpose in this lifetime, to reach their own pinnacle of success, enjoyment, adventure. We seek to share this joy with the world.

Each person who sees beyond their own horizon, who knows that humanity is in need of strengths shared, contributes to the gathering of warriors for the future wellness of Planet Mother Earth. Each person may think only of their own lives and family, careers, and interests, but as each person elevates their own wellness and functioning, the result is felt far and wide.

Working through limits and allowing the illumination of your life story can be a solitary experience, you might think. But you are never alone when your Higher Self is along for the journey. You will feel this love deeply and know it is the wind beneath your wings while on this Journey to Wellness and always.

The Joy of Discovery

We go now directly into the reason each person has for wanting to know what happened to them in past lifetimes. Each person has a willingness to undertake this journey and a certain measure of tolerance for the pathway itself. There are those who are cautious, who do not allow any discomfort in their psyche. Others are willing to dive deeply into the experiences that shaped them. It is in the examination and exploration of personal reasoning that we find the keys for each person's success. We intend for each person to find their selves healed. While "healing" is a strong word, it has differing meanings for those who need it. One person's healing is not another's.

To merely diffuse or deflect what was, that is not healing. Yet, there are those for whom these tactics seem like solutions. For others, it will be the total viewing, examination, and understanding of previous times and places that enables their release. While we feel the urgent need for healing across Planet Mother Earth, we accept that there is a solution for each individual, and know it is theirs to determine.

It is for each to understand that they are not alone in this lifetime and to know their inner strength is supported by Spirit, their Higher Self, and inner Soul Knowingness on their journey through life. That is the support team each person has, if they will open to it.

—Pax

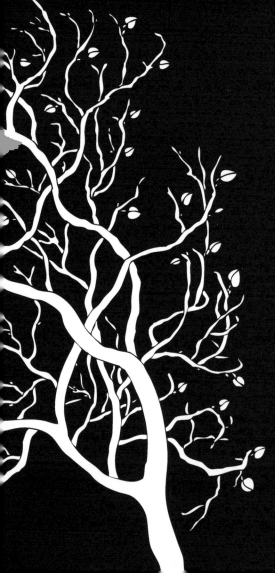

04

Recognizing Spirit Guidance in Your Life

It is time now for people to use all the tools they have to find wellness in their lives and recognize that Spirit is with them. There are troubles and challenges in life that can be met with resistance or understanding that we are not alone. How to recognize this?

Each person has to quiet their selves and become aware of the difference between their intellect thinking and their heart feeling. "Follow the heart we say," for in balance is wellness.

We suggest that an understanding that each person has the ability to speak with or receive guidance from their Higher Self is the beginning. That realization comes with the need to feel this energy within and allow it to be felt and heard. It is in one's thoughts, often, that spirit guidance is heard also in the heart, hence the reason for quieting one's self to receive.

A person needs to believe they have inner guidance, trust in it, and welcome it. With this combination, there can be communication. With this communication comes guidance. It is for each of you to accept, access, and absorb.

Trust in self and Self

We suggest that the exercise of listening and receiving, feeling and accepting is new to many people and may not seem like something they are capable of. We ask those questioning their selves to place more trust in their inner strength. Consider this an exercise in growing within, adding another life skill, and developing an inner strength you may not have considered possible.

It is for each to understand, or open to understanding, that you are not alone in this lifetime and are able to know inner strength is supported by Spirit, by Higher Self, and by Soul Knowingness on how to proceed through life. It is the support team each person has if they will accept and open to it.

We leave this decision to each person who wishes to make a difference in the level of happiness, contentment, and comfort they experience in their life today. Moving into the process and placing each person in control of their journey, this brings a peaceful beginning to finding wellness. We do not question the need for each person to decide when they are finished with their seeking – this is a personal decision and not to be questioned. What we do wish to share is the joy in knowing each person enters this healing journey in peace and understanding, that they do this for their selves, that healing is their right, and that peace is their fulfillment and destination.

We share the joy, your joy, and bring light and love from the Universe to each person's Path to Wellness.

Each person has the power, their own personal
power, with which to begin this process
and make change in their lives. To know this
is empowering – to act upon it is liberating.

Feeling this and knowing this inspires myriad epiphanies, and then the search deepens internally. It is at this time that awareness will increase to the extent that change comes to our thinking about spirituality, about personal reality, and about the significance of living in the moment and all that entails.

To be truly present in time and place, one must be accepting of one's personal make-up, one's DNA, and one's creation. Limitations not understood, such as those stemming from past life connections, can be investigated, and put to rest. That is achieved through recognition of how challenges can be a trigger response to past experiences.

Every person is deserving of health and happiness in life. This should be considered an inalienable right for all. But how many of us consider health and happiness to be a state they are deserving of? Too often, these gifts are seen as fringe benefits and what other people have, not something to strive for our selves. It is this giving away of personal power that is the beginning of a downfall: one that takes a person from viewing their self as owning their own future to one who considers their future questionable at best. Placing focus on the needs of others is a noble act, but when pursued to the detriment of one's own wellness it is folly.

At this point in the cycle of healing, we suggest the formula includes elevating one's own perception of self, or Self. Each person has a daily self and a Higher Self. The latter contains Soul Memory and travels with the person through all lifetimes, imprinted with the actions of past times and presenting those memories when they are accessed.

It is in the joy of discovery that a seeker comes to the realization that there is more to life than this life.
~Pax

Here is where we begin viewing our records of past experience. Here is where we select and isolate those episodes that have left their imprint on our daily lives. Here is where we release the attached emotion from those experiences and break the heavy chain linking today to the past.

When we envision each past lifetime as a link in a long chain of events, it is clear that one link can be removed without compromising the strength of the whole.

Our intention is to isolate and remove those links that do not serve us, while connecting and strengthening the links that do.

See the past

Feel the past

Believe the past

Release the past

There is a clear structure to this process, but the outcome is predictable. Know that you have full control to decide where and when you wish to investigate your past lifetimes, one at a time or in groups. These links in your chain can be approached at a time of your own making. This is the strength of the process – you can prepare for each session and set the guidelines accordingly.

See the Past

Here is where the line-up of past lifetimes is shown and where your inner Knowingness, your Soul Memories, will activate so that you can select the life and experiences you need to address. Or you may choose to enter this journey by asking your Higher Self, your inner guidance, to take you directly to the past lifetime most gravely impacting you today, where understanding and healing are critically needed.

As we view the time and place we found ourselves in during a past lifetime, and the person we then were, we can see how we were wronged, a common occurrence during that place in our history. We can identify those involved and know we are to extend understanding, forgiveness, and release of blame to them. We believe this and trust in this process, knowing that true forgiveness and severing harmful connections with the past are imperative for healing.

Feel the Past

We should be clear that the *feeling* aspect of a past life visit includes no discomfort, merely an awareness of what was. This sense of detachment is helpful in assessing the full scale of each experience in order to understand its place in time. You can view each experience as an observer, feeling what you will about it but not re-experiencing physical or emotional discomfort from that time and place.

Believe the Past

Recognize that what our circumstances were does not ultimately define who we were in a past lifetime. We were often an innocent victim of the times or of our status in life, without power needed to change the outcome. We succumbed to the control of others, and thoughts of personal power to improve our life shrunk to non-existence. We now believe in our Soul's goodness at that time and our deservedness of a better life, then and now.

Release the Past

Release and forgiveness toward the self we were then may also be needed. Do we have thoughts that, as that person we then were, we were responsible for harm to others, or that we could have done more to improve our own life? We should not direct blame toward that earlier persona of ours. Instead, we should extend kindness and understanding for the person we then were, releasing all but our healing love for them. This release will change how we move forward in this life and how we think about our history: ideally with love and acceptance for all we endured.

Emerging into Your Now

What a gift you have just given your self! Awareness begins to register the change, the difference you feel in all aspects of your physical and emotional wellness. Is there new peace in your mind and, even more so, deep peace in your heart?

When did you last know this absence of anxiety and presence of confidence together? These are the gift-wrapping you have placed on your inner change, the release of angst combined with the claiming of your own personal power. This shift in contentment brings newfound balance to your being. Spend time feeling it and knowing the joy of it. This is your celebration of Self.

Standing in your own light now, this is a state of mind where you embrace all that is your essence. It is here you recognize the calling of your strengths, your talents, and gifts to be acknowledged. For too long, too many people did not allow personal power to infuse their daily lives. Spirit has been seen as standing outside the reality of what is needed to get from one day to the next successfully. The truth is that only through embracing of one's gifts can we find fulfillment and inner peace. It is with this completeness that a person functions at their best.

Now that you have chosen to stand in your own light, reclaim your personal power, and allow in your greatness, there can be a bright new future for you that includes a clear and solid past on which to build.

Look to the Past to Find Your Future.

While there are many stages leading to wellness when opening the book of one's past, there is support and understanding from our Higher Selves, always. As we understand that we have had past lifetimes, and as we understand some of them have left us with challenges today, that same connection comes with love and the intention for this to be our best lifetime possible.

We are never alone in this or any journey. It is for us to understand that our inner voice, our intuitive Self, our Higher Power walking with us will ensure we know the way forward and keep our feet on that path. This is our Path to Wellness, and we will intuitively know the way and what is right for us at each moment in time. This is the beauty of being a Spiritual Warrior, and by that I mean a peaceful warrior on the journey to fulfillment of this life's purpose.

Healing Through Time

An important aspect of entering the Soul Healing process is understanding and belief that you are able to manage your own wellness, as people have been doing for millennia, and that you deserve wellness now and always.

It has been a reality through time that native plants were ingested and used as topical remedies. Today, crystals and energy healing continue use from ancient times. Combinations of naturally occurring medicinals were mixed and used widely to both prevent and cure. Dark magic played a role in belief systems and was widely used in many cultures. Tribal medicine is powerful, and many still value that knowledge in our current world.

Energy Healing and the Mind Body Connection

Throughout history, people have managed their own wellness (physical and emotional) as there were known remedies passed down from elders. Provided by the land, by a healthy environment, were naturally occurring plants capable of healing. There were elders whose life work was to know all there was to know about healing methods, to be a resource for people in need. Today, there is not such a healthy environment, but healing plants remain available to those who recognize them – that practice of healing continues.

Energy healing is a powerful modality, used by those who understand how meridians in the human body transmit energy and how they can become blocked, thereby creating dis-ease. The movement of this energy and releasing of blockages returns wellness to the body: a powerful practice indeed, and a testament to the mind-body connection.

Sound healing enables people to realign energy and return balance to the mind and body through vibrations produced by such instruments as crystal bowls. Bodies are comprised largely of water, therefore they sensitively respond to external vibrations being raised or lowered.

Natural healing comes in many forms that have been practiced for centuries. Collective energy put into an intention by masses of people at the same time, for a chosen purpose, can be effective in influencing outcomes. It is not new, this powerful energy healing method; it is ancient, having been practiced throughout history in mass meditation as well as varying forms of prayer.

The practice of mental preparation and strengthening is powerful. It brings positive intention and focused, results-based healing. The common expression "mind over matter" extends to mean that mental intention can overcome physical dis-ease. It is a practice of visualizing wellness, believing in wellness and how to achieve it, and intending wellness as the outcome. This practice of willing one's self to wellness is the basis of self-healing. To believe it will be, and trust it will be, sets up the positive mind-body connection for allowing it to be.

Heal the Heart, Heal the Mind, Heal the Body
~Pax

We say that "the body hears everything the mind says." This is evidenced in the strength of intention and conviction shown by those who manage their own wellness through positivity in thought and action. Theirs is the ability to visualize the desired outcome and move toward it in trust that it will be so. Of course, wellness comes in many ways and can be compromised in just as many. It is clear that taking all steps physically and mentally possible to achieve this wellness creates a harmonious result.

We share this knowledge in love and provide guidance based on Spirit Wisdom: that you may enter into the self-healing process in respect and trust for your self as well as your Higher Self, a piece of your personhood not always recognized or understood. This is your Soul Wisdom, your greater guidance and protector that has traveled with you through all lifetimes and continues, in this one, to watch over you. This is your peace and your joy in knowing you are not alone.

Becoming aware and capable of taking on the task of entering, with kindness, the sphere of a past life connection with intent to release the hurt: this is the way to acceptance and healing.

—Pax

05

The Soul Healing Process
Your Personal Power: An Inalienable Right?

Finding Your Bliss

Oh yes, we each have a life purpose to fulfill. In doing so, we find the greatest gift we can receive – the true blessing to be aware of what it is we are here to do, to accomplish, or gift to the world and humanity. We do not walk alone, nor do we walk aimlessly. We are to trust in our heart feeling that the path chosen is right for us. If it does not strongly resonate with your heart, then perhaps reconsider your choice of direction.

When we know we contribute to the betterment of our Planet Mother Earth, to humanity, and to our future as a viable society, then we can lead as intended. It may be that we are here on this Earth plane now to bring forward wisdom and guidance from another time and place, where we have been responsible for wellness of people and the planet. It may also be that we are a strong leader who is here to join a movement toward repairing this peaceful planet. We have a purpose here on Planet Earth, each of us, and it is in the recognition of this eternal truth, and undertaking the journey, that we find bliss. We ask each person to find their bliss, for it is in this discovery that your power is felt.

The Pathway Opens

It is only in this combination of knowing the past and the present that the future can be molded. Do you understand that there is bliss to be found and lived? Too often, daily living becomes routine and lacking joy, lacking inspiration, lacking fulfillment. Who can make the necessary change for each of you? Correct, it is a personal choice – as is everything in this earthly life.

Will you stand ready to accept the change that brings wellness in your present existence? It will require focus and strength and willingness to trust that your Higher Self will show you the past times that affect you negatively today. Just as importantly, your Higher Self will show you the way through to releasing the hold that heavy chain has on you, so that together you can remove the links no longer serving you. This process brings freedom from your past and the ability to move into your light of today, to feel that light and stand in it with strength and peace in your heart. This is owning your light and achieving the fullness of your being.

Now it is time to allow your greatness. What does this mean for you, going forward? It means that you have chosen the high road and chosen the path of healing for your self – not an easy path at times, but one which is taken in order to reach inner peace.

This means a commitment and desire to clear your mind and heart from energies carried for no useful purpose. Envision a screen filled with pictures of places and people and experiences that seem negative and also seem unrelated to you. This is the clutter of past energies maintaining themselves in your Soul Memories. They are always present and color your thoughts and actions without your awareness, or your permission. Think of that! This clutter of interferences can be cleared by your intention.

It is our joy to show the way to this process, whereby there can be recognition and forgiveness and releasing of what is not of value to your present or your future. This will be you emerging, like a butterfly from the caterpillar's cocoon, into the light of your power.

This may sound simplistic; it is, and it is not. The steps taken through this process may be somewhat simple. But the mindset needed, the trust and belief in your self as deserving of the best, this can be complicated for some. You will not be alone on the journey, as your companion, your loving coach, and Higher Self, ensures success on your chosen Path to Wellness.

Stages of the Soul Healing process:

- We visit your pertinent past lifetimes to learn who you were and the source of your current challenges.
- Through healing of those old wounds (by understanding, forgiveness, and release of the past) you become free to make your own wise choices and move ahead in wellness.
- Recognizing personal strengths brought forward from your past lives brings deeper self-awareness and growing empowerment.
- New and liberating responses to old triggers are created, resulting in greater personal power, heightened self-worth, and control over your present day body and mind.
- Guiding you to access the strength of your Higher Self taps into your Soul Power, leading to healing and personal transformation.

Transformational Path to Wellness

Do you meditate? Too many of us must answer "no." And that is because of all the barriers that hold us back. Meditation requires complete concentration and a mastery of breath, focus, visualization. In the modern world, these are unfamiliar skills. The Soul Healing process offers an alternative path, which allows for travel to your past lifetimes without heavy requirements. For now, we ask that concentration be placed on your heart – not the muscles themselves but the feelings in your heart. These are reactions to what you think. It is what you think that leads to what you feel, and it is within your body that these feelings are felt.

> *The body feels everything the mind says.*
> *~Pax*

Consider your physical reaction when you think of a person or place or animal you are very fond of. Do you feel, in and around your heart area, the warm-and-fuzzy reactions of love and pleasure? Then, think of what you most fear. Notice the heart feeling grows cold and unsettled in response to fear or dislike.

It is this communication between your body and your mind that we call on for visiting your past lifetimes in need of repair and healing. It is your inner knowing that allows for this journey through your past, visiting the places in those lifetimes that you do not consciously recognize, but your heart-knowing does.

Now we enter into the preparation for your Journey to Wellness: a time of peace and trust. You must trust in your Higher Self to lead you well, and trust in your consciousness to guide along the prescribed path. This is a pivotal time in your life; be in the moment and enjoy the experience.

You will not feel discomfort in the present from your past, as you travel and visit now as an observer only. We allow for you to see and to recognize a connection, a link between a past scenario and a present challenge in need of release and healing. In this way, we work through your past lifetimes and history, selecting what resonates with you as feeling connected or troublesome.

In your self-guided journey, you can view one or a series of experiences without prompting emotional responses. The goal is recognition of those past traumas that need your examination and understanding of their connection to your current life challenges. It is in recognizing these connections that you can consciously direct your Higher Self to remove the link between then and now as you see, understand, and forgive those involved. Breaking a link by releasing the connection, sending those involved away in love, and knowing your present and future are cleared of all related limitations – this is the light that comes from each clearing of your self, by your self, while growing your personal power in love and blessing.

It is the inner journey that is rewarding, always, and this is a fine example of getting to know one's self better and more deeply than ever before. Who would have thought that one day you could be looking back through time, across the decades, across the lifetimes and centuries, to connect who you were with who you are? Perhaps this thought would have been totally foreign to you. After all, it is a common ideology today that one life is all there is. We hear the phrase "you only live once" frequently, although that would be a tragedy if true.

At this time, we share that the many lifetimes offered for view are totally within the control of each person. Do you wish to return for your own specific reasons? This is a personal choice and falls within the guidelines each individual will determine for their selves, in their blueprint for their current lifetime. Will they simply do what they do in a lifetime and disappear? Or will they recognize there is more to experience and contribute, then apply their given energy to put in place a plan for a stronger return into bodily form, for the next go around? As we know that everything in life is choice, so we know that returning to life as a strengthened self is choice.

There is talk of Karma being responsible for people needing to return to right a wrong or pay a penance. There is also the reality of choice playing out for the love of it, and the good of it, only. The process for accessing a past lifetime is one we will guide you through in peace and joy.

There is a stillness needed in your heart, your mind, and your body. When this is found, there will be thoughts and words, each created and spoken for the purpose of placing you in a receiving and open mindset. When you reach your place of comfort, we provide the words and thoughts useful to envisioning your journey to your Higher Self, where access will be granted to the pertinent past lifetimes responsible for current life challenges.

While past life experiences are being shown to you, there will be no hurt or repetition of suffering experienced then. You are cocooned in Spirit and protected from pain and discomfort. You will view long-lost experiences only as an observer, so they may be recognized as connected to your current life challenges. In this way, the link is viewed but not felt as a trigger point for unwanted behaviors. This emotional distance is necessary for clearly seeing the connection and recognizing a past experience as needing your attention and release.

As you identify people responsible for hurt and trauma from a past time, you may also begin to recognize and understand why they acted poorly towards you. The intention is for you to let go of that link in your life chain by understanding, forgiving, and releasing those involved, including your self of that time. Allowing forgiveness to envelop you, as part of your intentional healing, this is liberating, empowering. It resets your connection to past influences.

The First Steps Taken

The regression process is designed to allow ready access to pertinent past lifetimes for each person. The intention is for Soul Memory to be accessed for the greater good and for the results to be life-altering positivity and joy. It is with the realization that this is our intention that we move forward in the creation of a new life. We do this today.

The roadmap for moving toward wellness includes a notation of where you are presently, with an extension to where you would like to be marked out in the margins. That is your destination of choice.

What no mere map, or blueprint, can show is the past: where you have been, the point of origin for you on this life path. The past is available and accessible, and a joy to experience as a catalyst for present life healing. Being led by your Higher Self ensures protection on the journey forward into your past. This is the starting place in your journey, now.

It is understood that the contemplation of this spiritual reality is likely new for many, and time is required for processing and becoming comfortable with it prior to beginning the journey. By this, we mean that each person who may not have considered they have had past lifetimes now needs to come to terms with the notion that they have had them. Further, those past lifetimes contain connections and triggers that reach far out through time to create challenges today. When this is understood and accepted, you can engage with the Soul Healing process as a tool for healing.

We know that unless we recognize the root of a problem we are unlikely to solve that problem. The same is true for current lifetime impediments to happiness, which are rooted elsewhere. Until we can connect today's triggers to past experiences, we continue to miss that vital piece of the healing puzzle: the key to wellness.

The greatest achievements begin taking the first step, and sometimes the greatest achievement is in taking that first step.

When this understanding has settled into your heart wisdom and bodily knowledge, and trust in the connection is in place, the process may begin. Regression into past lives should be seen as a natural progression, moving into these many lifetimes. Know that each has contributions to make for your present self. That knowledge can be deeply comforting. The wisdom and experience brought forward, as Soul Memory from past lifetimes, creates in you a depth of character that is a blessing. It is often accompanied by a sense of calm but powerful knowing, which we refer to as an innate Knowingness. This depth of wisdom is a gift and is to be acknowledged and trusted. It is not a gift possessed by all. Not yet.

We are enabled to separate today's life path from our past lives. Most importantly, we can separate the emotion related to past wounds from our life today, forgive and release what we once knew, and move ahead in freedom to be the person we desire to be. Separation from the past and transformation into the empowered you of tomorrow means healing and growing. Given the tools for making change, you can create your own Transformational Path to Wellness.

Identifying your pertinent past lifetimes reveals the triggers felt today as responses. Moving into the healing path of forgiveness, and releasing of our past selves from blame, this brings regained personal control. Affirmations for wellness further strengthen the awareness of self-healing and renewed physical and emotional health.

When we are triggered, we become who we think we need to be to survive. When we are constantly triggered, our personality changes to adapt. We live always ready for the next assault, which defeats the goal of inner peace.

Lightness of Being – Found

Truly separating our present life from our past allows for transformation. There will be gratitude for strengths and lessons learned from our past selves. Often, those blessings from the past bring us the necessary structure and stamina to follow our present Journey to Wellness. Changing life habits is never easy, but when we understand the triggers to our unconscious behavior we are empowered to create a process for growth and change.

Planting personal power seeds is an integral part of the healing process. Believing in one's self is the key to accomplishing anything in life, from the smallest first step to the greatest achievement. Often that achievement is in taking the first step.

Growing into the person we want to be entails being comfortable in our own skin and in our choices and surroundings. Truly feeling appreciation for our strengths, and even weaknesses that we have identified, this is empowering – as is recognizing our progress.

On our Path to Wellness, we feel the support that comes from our Higher Self. We feel the progressive healing of our mind and body and transition into feeling purposeful, in control, and grateful for our renewed self. We have gratitude for the abundance in our life and feel blessed that our inner strength and wisdom grows.

The ability to live well, without interference from our past life experiences, brings a lightness of being and release of fear.

Through the healing of our Soul, that which travels with us through lifetimes holding the highs and lows of past experience, we can rise above limitations and challenges and grow into our full and loving potential.
~Pax

Meeting Your Past: What to Expect

What we outline here is just that, an outline of how the process of regression appears, whether self-guided or in a guided setting. More detailed guidance for your journey is shared in the Process pages found later in the book.

We ask for trust in this process to find your wellness. It is the intention of your Higher Self to facilitate your return to happiness and freedom from subconscious triggers that control behaviors and reactions. Their origins are far back in time, and the links to your present should be understood but not felt, not suffered again. Here, we intend for you to have peace and harmony in your life.

While Soul Healing is in no way a simplistic process, there are basic steps to success:

- Visit a pertinent past lifetime's traumatic experiences.
- Identify the link to today's trigger responses.
- Recognize, understand, forgive, and release from blame the connected people and events.
- Feel and affirm your current wellness.

Much more than that will take place along the stages of your journey, but if you can be comfortable with this process then you will recognize the steps as you progress.

When you have identified a specific current challenge for your self, one which you are not able to control, we may proceed by visiting the past life where the cause originated. This is an intention and a choice and a pathway you can visualize in your mind's eye as one leading to healing.

Visualizing the Journey

- Ensure that you are in a quiet place, in your body and mind, with the intention of finding the place and time you need to visit. It is then, as you sit quietly and peacefully, having emptied your conscious mind of daily concerns, that you can ask your Higher Self to guide you in this quest to identify the past life source of your current challenge. Hold in your heart and mind the connection to your Higher Self while undertaking this journey. You will be protected along the way from straying off the chosen path. Focus on the challenge where you have asked for clarity.
- Allow your quiet mind to receive images along the pathway to the place you are guided to visit.
- When you arrive at a scene where you recognize your self, possibly in a situation of discomfort, this is when you are to watch and learn the situation as it was. You will not become attached to that past self or feel painful emotions of that time. You return only as an observer. Witnessing the situation that led to your enduring trauma reactions will be like watching a play with your self in a pivotal role. You will feel no discomfort while becoming aware of who the players were that created trauma for you. It is important to understand the situation, why it occurred, and the role you played in the outcome.

- Having come to an understanding of that scene and your role in it, you are positioned to release your self from connection between it and your present life. It is important to speak your forgiveness for each person that played a part, your past self included. Ensure you are sincere in the meaning of forgiveness. Send them love and healing energy. Infusing them with love and healing is the way to forgiveness from you to the people of that time and place, releasing them forever from blame and removing the pain of their actions from your Soul Memory.
- Before leaving that lifetime, you may feel there are other episodes needing attention. If so, place your focus there and ask your Higher Self to show you the picture of another situation in that lifetime you need to address. Repeat the process to recognize, understand, forgive, and release what no longer serves you, to enable your clear path forward into wellness.

You may have multiple challenges to be addressed and feelings of connection to places in time where you have lived. Countries and cultures that call to you, and periods in past centuries, signal that there have likely been influential experiences lived in those times and places.

These feelings of connection can be of happy and fulfilling lives as well as times of pain and suffering. Both are valuable to explore, as personal strengths, gifts, and talents are also brought forward to the present. Often, these are accepted without understanding, and to receive the full benefit one should witness their origins. Your Higher Self is your guide to viewing your past lifetimes of accomplishments and accolades that contribute to your present lifetime's strengths and abilities. To know your origins in this way is a testament to the you of those past times and acknowledgement of your dedication to learning and sharing those gifts today. There could be revelations regarding how navigating your life path of today mirrors those past times. Always there are lessons to be learned.

There are variations on the theme of how to approach this journey into your past, and whatever feels most comfortable can become your most effective method. Looking back in time and recognizing a pull to a specific time and place is one way to move into the past.

Visualize and feel your self looking within your heart for feelings and within your mind for thoughts that match each other. The experiences in a past life that inspire a sense of connection are real. We ask you to place your focus there.

Do you feel a familiarity with a place in geography and a point in time? Is there a pull toward it – and a need to know more? Open your heart, let it expand to go within your self, to feel the pull as it becomes like a stage play in front of your eyes. You see and feel the you of that time. You will know it by your feeling, know that your heart will recognize the you of that time.

When you see your self in a past lifetime situation, note where you are and if there are others with you. Note the circumstance at that moment, because you are being shown a pertinent experience that continues to affect you today. Is there conflict or negativity that concerns you? Is there an action taken against you that is hurtful? Note who is present and their relationship to you. Ask your Self if you recognize them as people in your world today. It often happens that those unresolved circumstances from the past carry forward, with people who played a part following each other through time in order to correct wrongs.

Do you have a clear picture of the conflict in which you were a victim or possibly an aggressor? You will want to imprint this experience on your present memory, so you can develop the needed forgiveness of those people. All those responsible for bringing pain and suffering to you at that time are to be forgiven. This is an important aspect of the process, as only in understanding and forgiveness can there be release, by you, of the hold this experience has had over your subconscious mind. The entire picture in that stage play can then be erased, as if the curtain had come down. Like writing on the wall of your heart, it can be deleted – leaving you in peace. You can release the connection from that lifetime. Visualize a cord being severed or a link being removed from the chain of Soul Memory. Then, send away in love those who participated in your harmful experience from that time.

Victory is yours in this battle against the sands of time that want to sweep across your present and change the outcome of your life. Not so fast, we say to those who still hold control over you today, based on an experience from your distant past. There is to be release and healing, returning happiness, and harmony. Remember that you control and deserve this outcome.

There is wisdom now and greater understanding of the process, so that each time there is a raising to the surface of past life negative connections, a step forward can be taken to address that trauma and effect the change needed for release. Visiting corresponding lifetimes to understand and release trigger points is done at your own discretion and in your own time. You will feel a need to take a step back in time and will be prepared, with the tools of the Soul Healing process, to make needed changes in your past and present. Your Higher Self as guide will always be up for the journey when you are. Trust in this and know the best is yet to be.

Affirmations for Wellness

The next step on the Path to Wellness is speaking affirmations aloud. To complete the circle of identifying, recognizing, and neutralizing past life trigger responses, clearly affirm that you are released from that connection, and believe it is so.

If the use of affirmations is not a regular habit, now is the time to grow into it by regularly speaking words of wellness to your self, your body, and mind. Enjoy the feeling of recognition. Yes, we say recognition, as there will be a visceral reaction: a feeling that the body-mind connection hears and rejoices in positive affirmation.

Say the following affirmations aloud, paying attention to which phrases resonate most strongly in your being:

- I allow my self to release the past and step into my light.
- I have been released to move forward in wellness.
- I visualize and feel my present self healed of past wounds.
- Those past life experiences are gone and have no power over me today.
- I am healed of past wounds and memories.
- I am in control of my life and my body and my mind.
- I visualize and feel my self in prime physical and emotional health.
- I make wise choices to honor my self.

These are just some of the infinite affirmations you can choose from. Choose to repeat those that resonate with you strongly. All affirmations are powerful and interchangeable. They will serve you well on your Path to Wellness.

When affirmations are spoken in love, from your self to your Self, magic happens. There is acceptance and belief and trust in these words coming from your heart. Remember, it is the heart that guides and the head that follows. If you live by this dictum, trust in it, and find peace with it, there will be forward motion in your life, leading to wellness beyond your expectations. Trust in this truth.

So powerful is this past life connection that it remains, through time, undiminished and unexplained, while continuing to haunt a person with no clarity as to its origin.

It is personal power that is the healer, and it is you who controls the wielding of this power.

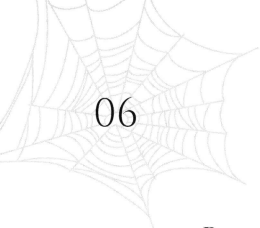

06

Recognizing Origins of Current Dis-Ease
This Lifetime or Another?

It is the time of rewarding, yes? There has been much concentration involved in determining the best steps forward for healing the past and present. These are the two powerful places for the Soul to be, and each has the power to influence what was and what is to be.

Now we ask each person to recognize that what is within them, in their hearts and minds and in their Souls, is what guides them into wellness, when the Soul is permitted to be heard. Yes, heard.

The inner voice that each of us has, the one guiding if permitted to do so, this is the innate Soul Wisdom that will always be present and can be trusted to have your best intentions, always. Giving stillness to a situation, allowing an opening for hearing and feeling and considering what is heard and felt, this is a behavior to be cultivated.

We have spoken of the penchant for allowing intellectual guidance to rule. There should be balance in life and decision making. To allow the heart to speak and wisdom of the Soul to come through, this will provide that balance. It is then those wise choices can be made, as it is then that all necessary guidance will have been heard.

Using all available tools is a good decision when approaching a task.

When that task is making important decisions, then for certain it is wise. Taking personal power into consideration, as one of the available tools, brings a new dimension to the equation. As we speak of inner wisdom, so do we equate it with personal power, for one is based on the other. In life, there are many available options and going within or going without is always your choice. We speak to you now of the joy of going within, for this is where you find who you are, truly.

Each time there is a decision made based on your own personal knowledge, feelings, and intellect, you build that muscle further – that muscle of personal strength and wellness that grows and intensifies and becomes more valuable to you. This is your way forward, this inner strength, and this is your way back also, back to tackle, in love, that which has left you compromised in this lifetime. You now know that whatever transpired in the past is no match for who you are now, today, in your resolve to repair and renew your current life.

You are not alone, as we have said. The Universe supports and guides your journey. Angels smile at the opportunity to lift you to the task ahead. It is now yours to undertake. Step onto the path you have chosen. This will prove to be the most important journey you take and the one with greatest value to your present as well as your future selves.

Stepping into your light, into your strengths and abilities, this is not a place of comfort for many. Why is this, we ask. Think of all that is required for Soul Healing. It is trust, yes? Trust in self and also in the Higher Self are required. Often, there is a wish to allow another to make decisions and choices and give us direction. This requires no personal accountability in the end. Following a path prescribed by another takes many through their lives, and at no time is there accountability for a wrong turn. If that turn was prescribed by the leader but proves to be a wrong turn for the goal, it is someone else's error. This is a way of going, yes. But is it a way of building personal belief in self, personal trust, or personal strength? We say the answer is clear.

Take the high road and allow the process to become one with you. Allow for the taking of chances and making of choices to become your way forward. It is only in this step that you feel the joy of personhood, the full range of emotions that bring feeling and appreciation of Self.

Always there is the option of proceeding or halting to regroup, slow and steady, and in this case, moving forward into the past to build your future, your wellness, and trust in self.

Emotional and Mental Health Challenges

Behaviors that are uncontrolled – such as addiction to gambling, drugs, and alcohol; or depression, criminal activities, and anxiety; abusive behavior toward self and others; or even hatred and racism – these can be leftovers from past life conditioning. They can be removed from the patterns of this life through the Soul Healing process. It takes awareness and recognition, understanding and willingness to address the who, when, and why of it all. Only then – after recognition, understanding, forgiveness, and release of that experience into the ethers of time – only then can you break free from lingering effects and fill that inner space with peace and love.

Going forward there is to be a permanent epiphany. You will recognize this as a process you can use in many instances in life. Nobody controls your life but you – or at least nobody should be permitted to do so, not even the past you from another lifetime, a different person in different circumstances who cannot know what is best for you now.

So, reclaiming personal power and choosing the course for this current life path is up to you. This action is supported by your Higher Self, always. Claiming personal power and stepping into your light is a most important forward step. Trust in this truth.

Where Does Hatred Originate?

This poisonous emotion seems to be prevalent in today's world. Thoughts, words, and actions are all in need of healing. Yes, healing.

It is a deep-seated emotion, hatred, and one which people are not born with. Or are they?

Investigating the origin of strong emotions that we do not fully understand can reveal trauma imprinting from a past life. When they become lodged in our DNA, past experiences, traumas, teachings, and conditioning are as integral to a person's character now as when first experienced. Born without hatred in our hearts, we are also born with the predisposition for strong emotions to remerge when triggered by current events.

This is indeed a triggered emotional reaction, this showing of hatred. As it is internalized wherever it grows and festers, the emotion can be diffused through understanding and through allowing in the light of recognition. This leads to release. We say this combination results in healing, although it is a process of developing the necessary steps to an end result – all very rational and logical and doable.

Where Does Fear Originate?

Irrational fear of such things as heights, abandonment, death, intimacy, failure, illness, poverty, and animals can be attributed to Soul Memory from the past. So can any irrational phobias that do not originate in this current life.

Indeed, experiences from the past can impact the experiences of today greatly. How is this possible? Conditioning from another time. It is strong and powerful still, this Soul Memory that may have come from many lifetimes, or only one. But if a past life has included an untimely death, then perhaps those circumstances remain in memory. Was it a fall? Did man or animal attack? Illness? Crash? A drowning? Whatever the experience, lingering fear of it recurs and remains strong. But it goes unrecognized and misunderstood without awareness of its origin.

Fear can rule a life. It is that powerful! It prevents us from moving forward in varying degrees, from an inability to mingle with other people to an inability to leave home for fear of injury. There is refusal to take common means of transportation, fear of germs and disease, avoidance of animals, and the obsessive need to examine all minute details of a situation for fear of being tricked or robbed. Some refuse to trust or be close emotionally to others, and they constantly question everything with the view that something will harm them. It is crippling, this fearful affliction. Yes, we see it as affliction, for it does not allow for free-flowing energy and joy in living. This we can change and this we can alleviate. This we can heal. Or rather, you can heal your fears with blessings from the Universe. We share the view behind the curtain, so that the next act of this play that is your life becomes cleared of obstacles.

Where Does Depression Originate?

Here we have another very personal inability to regulate emotional wellness, which of course leads to instability of physical wellbeing. Looking into past lives can reveal perceived failures and even deaths resulting from actions taken by others. While our past selves had no means then to fight back or retaliate. The unfortunate deaths of past selves now symbolize failure of the individual and the causes they championed in their own time. We err by observing our past failures – in this life or others – without leniency and compassion that recognizes the reality of past circumstances. When blame is laid by the person of today on the person they once were, this clouds their view of the past and the present.

Past lifetimes can be complicated to examine and to evaluate, for there are many moving parts, many people involved, and totally different cultures, lifestyles, customs, laws, beliefs, and truths to consider. When a past persona was charged with the responsibility of fulfilling a role they did not agree with, there was often no recourse but to comply or die. Living life as a lie was often the only means of survival, and that shame stays within Soul Memory. To not function at a high level of competency or happiness, but with allegiance to unchosen masters of the time, this left our past selves unfulfilled. It is understood that the expectation to serve and obey without question was the requirement of many, often on pain of death.

Many people today have felt this need for loyalty, without possessing an understanding of its source. The misplaced allegiance of past times can come forward in a need to find clarity in all details of life that touches us today. There is cleansing to be done and release of self-criticism for past choices. Very often, life does not offer choices other than "do or die."

Do you have, today, a strong need for respect? A need for personal integrity and balance in what is asked of you and what you are willing to provide? Yes, of course. Your Inner Knowing includes feelings of not being true to your self – a most uncomfortable knowing. As healing begins and trust in self and the Higher Self grows, there is a stepping into the role of a healthy and aware citizen of our times.

Where Does Anger Originate?

Anger is carried in the heart, not the mind. It is an emotion fraught with intricacies and is unusually close to the Soul, in spanning from then to now. Who has not been hurt or inflicted hurt upon another? Or both? Who has not been hurt over time? It is in the recognizing of what was intended to do harm – versus what was simply an innocent comment made or action taken in passing – that one can reflect and release the remnants of those past words and deeds. For those who carry a deep-seated anger within them, this healing is not easily managed.

How can we let go of our resentments? Anger and resentment are one, and recognizing this and leaving behind the picture of past experience can eradicate the need to continue the punishment. We understand that punishment is inflicted on both sides when a past injustice, perceived or real, is dredged up in memory with the intention of retribution. This is a bad idea. No good comes from holding a hateful thought within, especially one connected to the wish to hurt others. Retaliation is a function of war, and it should never be deployed person-to-person when forgiveness and release would clean and clear the heart and allow in peace and love. Herein lies the solution.

For the person going through this present life with impatience, disrespect, animosity, and an inability to be accepting of others – this is your wake-up call! Where does your rage originate? How damaging has it become to your emotional and, yes, physical health and wellness?

The negativity of anger is well known to permeate the physical as well as emotional being. When it endures, it contributes to dis-ease. This emotion is self-defeating, counter-productive to healthy living, and it can be traced to unresolved experiences from the past. Exploration of these feelings is valuable and can show that the you of today is a victim of traumatic, past life experiences. You did not come into this life aware of these negative character traits; they are found within your Soul Memory. They can be accessed along the journey of exploration, can be recognized as triggers, and then released.

What a relief that would be to your present life. Self-preservation requires good mental health and wellness as well as knowledge that you are cleared of what no longer serves you, was not intended to become you, and was an unintended consequence of a past life or lives. This is the healing release you will experience through following the Soul Healing process, a transformational journey into the truth of your being.

Where Does Addiction Originate?

Well now, here is a multi-faceted and complex set of irregularities in a person's make-up. Through time, there have been explorations of this condition, and the many realities of historical times show that people living in hardship were prone to look for escape or assistance, for help in getting through the days. They groped for a crutch to dull the pain, both real and perceived. The appetite for substances and penchant for poor habits began to surface and spread in their approval and use.

Dulling or numbing the senses to alleviate pain became common through the use of plant-based elixirs, tonics, and substances to be ingested or smoked to allow for distancing from reality. Liquor, hallucinogenics, and smokables were crutches to evade or postpone the inevitable reckoning with Self, as they still are today.

Dangerous substances or negative behaviors that allow the conscious mind to be dulled or temporarily removed from a troubling situation, or from life in general – these seem to serve as an aid that can be relied upon, and therefore rationalized.

Gambling, for example, is a recreational drug for some – but a desperation measure for others who seek solutions beyond their grasp. The false hope of effortless monetary gain is often seen as a means to solve problems and achieve personal wellness. Based on our historical giving away of personal power in past lifetimes, the default to seeking solutions outside one's self now becomes a compelling way of life.

Current day addictions, intended to blur reality, can be linked to the choice of discounting thoughts that personal power can overcome adversity. It is a matter of belief in self, belief in Self, and trusting both sufficiently to look within for strength and guidance.

Where Does Anxiety Originate?

Paying attention to where and when anxiety appears in a current lifetime leads us to explore the why, also. Understand that the chain of attachment to past lifetimes ensures that feelings remain strong, palpable, and bring with them a deep sense of living out traumas now. We know that this connection is not yet fully recognized by the you of today. Therefore, healing is difficult; how do we heal what is unknown to us? We provide the process, and each person may access this and choose to heal their own situation. Awareness is key. Does this mean reliving historical, personal trauma? No, it does not. That would only bring more pain. There is no need to revive past harms on your healing Journey to Wellness.

Anxiety today is a direct link to Soul Memory of past lifetimes.

Do today's events trigger emotions that reflect what once was? Is there a palpable connection between today and a specific set of circumstances or actions taken in a past lifetime? Or from more than one lifetime? Recognition of the link at Soul-level is a personal strength, but it can be inhibiting too.

When we consider our ability to go forward in this life – addressing daily challenges at work or at home and then realizing we have an unexplained inability to manage these challenges – this is the time to look deeper and beyond what is presented on the surface of your present moment.

Anxiety anchors your present to the past. In recognizing this unconscious connection, it can be diminished, diminished in favor of looking deeply within to find an explanation and solution to what that connection brings to your current life.

The direct connection from what is presented to you today and the origin of personal anxiety, this is where we ask you to begin your healing. It is the recognition and acceptance that there is a hidden connection that begins the Journey to Wellness.

Reaching back to view your past lives, see them as scenes passing in front of you. You will not be touched by the emotion of what you witness. That distanced position enables you to choose where to stop and look more closely at the people and places involved. It is important to recognize a situation or trauma as having contributed to your current life challenges, fears, and the inability to overcome them. When you see an episode clearly, you can become aware of where your understanding and release of blame for those involved is to be directed. This process is pivotal in bringing change to your life. Without understanding and forgiveness of the past, there will be no release of your present challenges. Without this acceptance and release, there remains a lingering shadow of what was. It can take time to work through this stage of the process – allow it time.

Recognizing and releasing the hold this has on you, the harmful incident from your past, this results in healing of that portion of both lifetimes.

This pathway opening to you is intended to provide access to understanding and healing that enables you to transform and emerge, like a butterfly from the cocoon, into the life you are destined to enjoy.

The Woman's Healing Journey

Beginning with the predicament of women, who seem to be the ones carrying the heaviest load in your present time, we speak of the journey they can take to identify what has landed them in a place of unwellness. With the intention of connecting current problems to their unknown source, we can go forward into her past, which is where we find her story revealed. We can reveal her story without asking her to re-live past pain. This approach to healing provides the best of both worlds. We can take her back in time to witness the trouble and trauma visited upon her, without the need for her to feel those past events. This is her protection against re-living pain. There is no need to re-experience pain, anxiety, or any negative emotions related to a prior trauma. On this basis, we can say the procedure is one of examination, not experience. We invite those who feel they will benefit from greater knowing to undertake Soul Healing.

Does not each person deserve a complete understanding of who they are and why? Your people look to ancestors and DNA to tell their story. Such evidence can relay who you are by blood. But how will you know your selves deeply in terms of your psyches? What deep and unanswered connections do your current selves have to events that trigger negative responses?

It is our wish to provide this view of history for each person wanting to witness, from a safe distance, their backstory. We offer this miraculous perspective as a gift to humanity. To reduce or relieve the need to carry past life experiences that are less-than positive, this is the gift from your Self to your self: the one trying to get through life without drama or unnecessary blocks. Having answers to the basics will assist with your Soul's healing.

The Man's Healing Journey

Now we look to the men of your world, the ones who feel pressure to be strong, in control, informed, and capable, always. Is this male dominance in action? Is this a male-dominated society making these demands? Is this a set of demands parents teach children, their little boys who are to grow into men always in control? If this is a standard, then it is a high one for the male to achieve. How is it that no leeway is given when it comes to a man's job, a man's duty, and a man's role to be a leader and protector? This false ideal is a danger for your world today, and too high a bar to be maintained in good emotional and even physical health.

Looking into the reality of your Earth time, it appears the male and female roles are reversing, somewhat. Such reversals are good and just when they are designed by those involved. True strength need not be measured by push-up prowess anymore; rather, it is a combination and compilation of attributes, ranging from physical and mental to emotional integrity. Without this balance, men are dragged back to former times and what was once considered the ideal man. From Neanderthal times to present day, each era values traits that were needed for a given time and culture. What a journey it has been to see this evolution in personal growth to suit the needs of the day.

Softening and melding of personal traits has taken place on your Planet Mother Earth, across civilizations, and the expansion of gender roles has now become commonplace. We address the roles that make up the change, how they have come to serve differing purposes that require differing strengths.

Recognizing Your Innate Wisdom

We go forward in the belief that your people today on Planet Mother Earth are doing their best to grow and function within their abilities and, for some, beyond them. We wish to offer assistance to all who feel there is more to life than their day-to-day experiences — work and family and growing up and growing old and continuing to strive for more. There are those who seek their inner wisdom and their spiritual guidance. It is to those people we wish to address our speaking today.

Going forward in your lives is a double-edged sword. On one side is the need for self-awareness and continued growth, while on the other is responsibility to family, work, and other areas where commitment has been made. There is often little room left for introspection and spiritual seeking and growth. It is this lack of prioritizing that concerns us, and we suggest that a reworking of the plan is in order.

You know the need to look after your own wellness first, so you can care for others. This is a fact of life too often overlooked. Do you understand that giving always to others, while a virtuous action, can leave you lacking and without personal resources to be the support for those who look to you for strength and guidance? Where is the line drawn between generosity and failure to recognize personal limits? Each of us has a line to draw in the sand: either remain on one's own side or continually step over it in service to others, thereby erasing one's own boundaries with footsteps in the sand to the extent it becomes illegible and unreal. This is not wise, helpful, or a contributor to the long-term wellness of all.

> *Not everyone recognizes that they have lived before this lifetime — not yet.*

How do we address those who have concerns about the reality of their own past?

Perhaps you have lived numerous times and come into this life with strengths as well as challenges carried forward from those past times. Current challenges could be irrational fears, compulsions, addictions, anxieties, suicidal thoughts, depression, substance abuse, PTSD, or uncontrolled anger. Also brought forward from past lives are extraordinary talents, strengths, wisdom, and other positive character traits. When past inheritances are recognized, this is the awareness-raising and pivotal moment that can result in a need for deeper investigation. Here is where we begin to support seekers with the blueprint for going forward into the Soul Healing process.

This journey into your past can be undertaken in private, in the comfort of a familiar place, and can be repeated as needed to access additional past lifetimes with healing intention.

When exploration of connections begins, it is common for seekers to recognize their selves in what they learn of their past lives, and that person they once were, seeing those influences in their present character.

Understanding and releasing the hold a past event has on you breaks the chain of connection from then to now and allows for healing.

07

Opening a Portal to Your Past: Visualization Techniques

Soul Memory – Your Personal Akashic Records

We speak of Cell Memory and the influence this has on your body and mind. Now we speak of this as Soul Memory and the greater power this has over your physical and emotional wellness. Soul Memory holds your personal Akashic Records, your blueprint of all you have witnessed and participated in throughout your history. This record is a key to your Spiritual Source and opening to grow that sacred relationship. Knowing this process allows for a Journey to Self and reclaiming of heightened personal wellness.

Each person has the opportunity to access this, their history, with their personal Guide by concentrating on breathing, quieting the mind, and asking for the presence of their Inner Wisdom, Higher Self, or their Guides, whatever the choice of description. We suggest that opening to the awareness of what passes through the mind in pictures and through the heart in feelings is also very important. There will be recognition sensed; follow where it leads.

The pictures that play across the screen of the mind now, follow them. Watch these scenes from your past roll by and allow the heart and mind to remain open to receiving what comes. This is needed for healing. A strong connection between then and now may be felt, so there should be awareness of all senses during this process. If you become aware of only one picture, one lifetime, one persona that you recognize, then this is the right destination for you on this stage of your journey. The scenes in your picture show may be from one lifetime only. If so, then this is where you are to focus your healing journey.

Do you know the feeling of recognition? Be aware of this, as it will be an indicator of where you are and were in your past life. How you feel as you see a character and scene will tell you if you are recognizing a scene pertinent to your present life experience.

Be aware of this powerful recognition, and do not discount the feeling when received – no matter how disconnected you may think the scene is from your current reality. Trust in this feeling, as the body will speak in the reactions you feel. Connections will become clear as you become attuned to your physical and emotional self.

You may choose to ask your Guides to take you directly to view a pertinent past life experience: one that is connected to your current life challenge and one you will benefit from understanding now. This is your choice to make. At no time while on this journey into your past will you go anywhere that is not beneficial to you. As part of your entry into the process, you will have put in place boundaries and protections. It is your journey, planned and fulfilled, to benefit you now and in your future.

We suggest that Soul Healing does not entail random seeking, but rather this is a gift to your self that you can undertake for distinct purposes. As we have said, your challenges – for example, fears of heights, animals, water, flying, sounds, or anything at all that unduly triggers you today – can be traced to actual occurrences in past lifetimes. These and other challenges can be connected to people in those past times who have harmed you, or people you may have harmed.

This process enables you to identify who you were at the time of trauma, and how you came to be in that situation. This understanding opens your communication with that past self. This allows you to recognize, understand, forgive, and release those involved in the events that left their mark on the you of today.

Were you harmed, or was there some profound incident that left you traumatized and unable to release the memory? It is these occurrences that can be addressed with a clarity through a process that brings an ability to release the trigger from your present self by neutralizing that situational memory.

We ask that you approach this process with reverence and respect for your current self, your past selves, and your Higher Self. That generosity will enable you to travel far on this Journey to Wellness, with Universal Wisdom supporting you along the way.

Visiting past lives is a process referred to as regressing, but we also refer to it as a Journey to Wellness. It is this journey, which each person undertakes differently, that leads to finding the essence of their true and best self. It begins with seeking and finding your true nature.

Going forward now in the description of this process, we say that it is not a simplistic journey, nor is it difficult. But it does take trust in your self, intention, and focus. It also takes patience, because one journey into your past may not provide all that is required to heal challenges, some of which have developed over centuries. As with many growing skills, practice and repeating the recommended exercises brings success and fulfillment. Some talents develop more slowly than others, but just as fully.

> *This pathway opening to you is intended to provide access to understanding and healing and enable you to transform and emerge, like a butterfly from the cocoon, into the life you are destined to enjoy.*
> *~Pax*

Opening a Portal to Your Past – Your Higher Self as Guide

I am blessed that my Higher Self guides me on the Path to Wellness and supports me in love, wisdom, and inner strength.

Look upon this process now as a gift you give to your self. Wrap this gift in the peace and quiet of a chosen place and time, where you will not be disturbed – where your surroundings are quiet and comfortable.

- Sit quietly and comfortably with feet on floor and eyes closed.
- Focus on breathing, only your breathing, in and out regularly – breathing in peace and calm, breathing out all cares of the day. Feel the peace and calm fill your body and mind. Allow tranquility to envelop you completely until you feel focused, relaxed, and ready to proceed.
- Feel the Earth's energy vibrations rising up through your feet, into your body, and circulating throughout. Visualize the cosmic golden energy cord extending from the heavens, down through the top of your head at your Crown Chakra – feel that energy flowing into your body, filling it with love and light. Visualize and feel this healing energy flowing through you from both sources: up from Mother Earth through your feet and down from the heavens through your Crown Chakra, to meet and fill your body, swirling and melding like a river flowing into and becoming one with the ocean.
- Feel the tingle of this healing energy being absorbed and imagine it, visualize it, filling your body, circulating, and settling in like a warm and gently humming presence.
- Feel the peace, feel the love, feel the calm.
- Ask for the presence of your Spirit Guides to be with you in love and protection on this journey into your past. Acknowledge your Higher Self as Guide and wisdom source.

- Visualize and feel this energy encircling you now, creating a glowing field of love and protection around the outside of your physical body. Know you are encircled by love and protection for your journey.
- Feel your Soul's connection with the power of Mother Earth and the Universal Consciousness. Allow wisdom and guidance to flow through you, as you to become one with your Soul.
- Begin breathing into your heart the intention to open your self to resolving a present life challenge by finding the source of it. Breathe in and out, focusing on the intention to recognize, understand, and heal.
- In thoughts or words, ask for your Higher Self to be your Guide in identifying the past life you most need to visit. Ask to visit that specific and pertinent lifetime connected to the challenge of today that you intend to understand and resolve. Ask to be made aware of the experience of that time needing your attention now and ask that your visit be as an observer – that no discomfort or negativity from that time be felt by you now.
- Open your heart to receive this guidance in thoughts, pictures, or feelings. Each person receives in their own way. As you do, focus and stay with what comes to you: as a picture in your mind or feeling in your heart. Begin to feel your past persona and see them in your mind's eye. Take time to settle in with this vision, or feeling, and be comfortable with this connection to the you of another time, with what you see, and what you sense.

Now enter the scene – you are an observer.

If more structured guidance would be beneficial, the following self-guided visualization technique can be used.

Opening a Portal to Your Past – Self Guided Visualization

This visualization exercise is designed to provide a staged progression into past lifetimes that are limiting your present wellness. Having already identified what in your present life needs understanding and healing, use this regression method to access your pertinent past lifetime, where a harmful connection originated.

Begin by settling into a comfortable and quiet location. Clear your conscious mind and ask for the presence of your Higher Self to guide and protect you on this journey. Sit comfortably with feet on floor and imagine a golden cord of light and protection entering through your Crown Chakra, at the top of your head, and then encircling you completely. Settle into this feeling of love and protection. Ask your Guide, your Higher Self, to take you directly to the pertinent past lifetimes responsible for today's need for healing, holding in your heart the current dis-ease.

You may progress through more than one lifetime on the way to wellness. Or you may choose to visit only one per session; the choice is yours.

Entering a Portal – The Elevator Method

- Visualize your self in a building, standing in front of an elevator. The door opens and you enter the elevator. You turn to see a panel of buttons with numbers on them. You make a selection by pushing a button for the floor you want to visit. The elevator descends, down through the numbers as you watch them count down, continuing to go lower and lower until reaching your chosen floor, where the door opens.
- You leave the elevator and see a long corridor ahead with doors on both sides. You walk forward along the corridor, knowing you will choose one of the doors to open. The doors are not marked.

But you will feel drawn to one particular door. When you do, you will open it and walk through.

- As you enter your chosen space, it may be a room or a forest, a village or a place that is filled with people. There may be activity, or it may be a tranquil scene. It may look familiar or not at all. You can move ahead or back in time by asking your Guide to move to the scene you need to witness. When you observe a scene that is familiar, you have entered a past lifetime of yours and one that is pertinent to your current life challenges.

- Notice what clothing you are wearing, for this helps identify time and place. Sense what you are feeling and if anyone in the scene is recognizable. If so, notice what actions are taking place and if you, as you were in that lifetime, are present.

- Allow your self to watch and be aware of the scene, like a play on a stage in front of you. Are you an actor in this play? Are there other people present? Do you know any of them? Do you sense good feelings or unhappiness? You will not feel discomfort at viewing this scene from your past, as you are present as an observer only: there to witness and understand.

- Is there a connection between this scene you observe and the challenges experienced in your current lifetime? If there is not an immediate connection, ask your Higher Self, your Guide, to move you forward or backward in time to locate the experience you will benefit from witnessing.

- Visualizing and feeling your self in this past life, as you were, will reveal much about that lifetime. Look also to where and what were your surroundings. Get a feel for the you and the circumstances of that time in the place you see. Does it look familiar?

- Is there a specific situation underway that you are involved in, or that you are observing? Perhaps you are alone in the scene. Do you see the potential for danger in any way? Are there others in your picture that are interacting with you? If so, notice your place in the story and what is coming your way. Is there something or someone you recognize that connects with your present day life?

- Begin to sense your emotions of the time; they translate now as thoughts and awareness. You will feel no discomfort as you view the scene as an observer. See the picture and where you are in it. View this as a stage play: a look into that lifetime and your place in it. What is the scene showing that relates to today's challenge? Focus on the scene playing out in your vision.

Talking to Your Past Self – A Healing Conversation

- Speak in thoughts or in words to the person you then were, asking for a description of what they are experiencing. You have the sense of being in both places simultaneously because you are. This enables your clear vision, while you remain protected from absorbing negative emotions from the past.
- Observe the situation and ask clearly how you are involved. What are you to learn from this experience? What message is embedded in it for you? Listen in your thoughts for the response. Be open to hearing or sensing the story. Perhaps dialog is not to be in this case, and your understanding of what transpired, and why, will come through intuition. This may be how you best receive your history. Either means of understanding will enable you to connect the awareness of that past experience to your present self. Is there trauma happening to you? Is there loss or sadness? Is there something causing fear to be felt? Is there an inability on your part to fulfill obligations or protect loved ones? Past trauma experiences triggered by today's events need to be examined and understood, for without true recognition of cause and effect there will be difficulty in finding resolution.

- Can you truly understand the circumstances of this past traumatic situation, your place in it, and its connection to your present day life? Is it sufficiently clear that you can relate it to your present day triggers? That connection provides the opportunity to receive clarity. Ensure enough time is devoted to the session to fully understand this connection. Your intuition, coupled with your view of a past situation, brings recognition of how your present is connected to your past, and a past lifetime in particular.
- This is where communication with the you of a previous time can bring clarity and allow for your next important step in understanding and accepting what was and releasing those involved from responsibility. It is with this release that you are able to begin the healing process. Those people can then be forgiven for their actions. It may be that forgiveness also needs to be extended to the person you were at the time, who may have acted badly toward others.
- When you are clear on this and understand the situation as it was and how it affects you today, then you can release the connection to that past experience. You can leave your past self with thoughts of love and understanding. You can also ask your Higher Self for guidance to move forward in your present life in wellness.
- To recognize and understand the picture you saw, feel the energy of the time, and release your connection to it. This is the intention. Speak your words of understanding and forgiveness, then release all involved with love. This step completes the process. Truly feel your words of understanding, release, and love. Hold the healing intention in your heart. This is your soulful commitment to the you of your past, present, and future.
- You now have clarity. Following the intention to remove that link in the chain of influence from past to present, you can move forward in trust that your Path to Wellness is cleared of this obstacle.

- Be thankful for the connection with your past self and extend gratitude for the clarity received. Your past and present selves have both chosen to release your connections, except where they can be beneficial for you today. You may also end your dialog with gratitude, love, and thanks for healing experienced.
- If you feel another lifetime requires visiting at this time, repeat the process of asking your Higher Self to show the way and identify your next past life visit. You may visit many lifetimes, and as often as you choose, to fully understand and release the sources of your current triggers and dis-ease. This is your journey and your choice.
- When ready to leave each session, extend gratitude to your Higher Self for guidance and protection during this journey. Then, formally ask your Guide to close the session with love and appreciation. It is a gift and blessing to make this connection and should be respected as such.
- Close by asking your Higher Self to shift your consciousness now to the present Turn your thoughts toward appreciation for the journey just taken. Ask that you return with clarity of mind and heart. Once wide awake, you feel rejuvenated and refreshed, deeply aware of the positive, profound changes you have made. Notice how light and relieved you feel.
- Take time now to truly appreciate how blessed you are. Following this session to connect with a past lifetime, there should be contemplation and quiet time to absorb what has been shown to you. This will be an extraordinary experience and, no doubt, it will come with a need for significant contemplation. You will benefit from time to consider the larger meaning of this new awareness, how it impacts your current life, and how it heals the past as well. One is connected to the other and both will heal. Less understood, but just as true, is the healing this brings to your future.
- Allow this experience, and what you saw and felt, to permeate your body and Soul now. You have been altered with this

knowing, added to, and enriched your being as a result. Time must be allowed to pass while the ensuing emotions settle within you. What has been felt and witnessed is a gift, and what has been learned will enable you to grow and heal within your current life's blueprint.
- Give your self the gift and the blessing of speaking affirmations to bring comfort and closure, to confirm your intention of going forward in wellness.

Healing Path Affirmations

- I have released and forgiven my past self with love.
- I visualize and feel my present self healed of past wounds.
- I am blessed that my Higher Self guides me on the Path to Wellness and supports me in love, wisdom, and inner strength.

More Past Lives, More Present Healing

At any time, you may visit and call upon additional past life identities of yours that are connected to present day challenges. Ask your Higher Self to guide you to the places where you may learn more of your history. It is beneficial also to learn how past lifetimes may intersect with each other. Family, friends, and even adversaries appear with you in successive or multiple lifetimes. Lessons are to be learned from these recurrent characters in the endlessly evolving story of your Soul.

You may feel the need to consult additional past life personas to understand their links to present day challenges. So, begin subsequent sessions in the same way prescribed in these pages and follow your chosen process. Close each past life visitation with gratitude and love as well as positive affirmations. Say the truth out loud: this was a gift for your past and present selves.

Recognizing, forgiving, and releasing the people involved in each traumatic scenario, your self included, is your pathway to breaking the chains of past life influence. This is your Path to Wellness: through understanding these connections and releasing the triggers and trigger responses of today.

We share with all present that the Higher Self, your Soul Wisdom, knows who you were, not just who you are.

—Pax

08

Liberation: Living Your New Story

Gaining a new lease on life – this is how the next stage is often described by those who have recognized and released the root causes of their present day dis-ease, challenges, and blocks to wellness and happiness. The phrase "life altering" also describes the experience, particularly for those who gained remarkable insight into their inability to function as they aspire to.

Experiencing past lifetimes using the Soul Healing process is a personal Path to Wellness. Each person can walk their path and use the wisdom gained from their experience to stay on the path. You may receive hints at what once was a block, or associated triggers. There can also be immediate recognition and release of that connection, that link needing to be severed. This is what the Journey to Wellness allows for, and it is a gift to those using this process to claim their freedom from past life shadows.

Wellness comes in many forms: physical, emotional, psychological, spiritual. It applies to all areas of life, without exception. We suggest that the gift of healing is one that belongs to all humanity. We share the process with love and intention for your reclaimed personal power.

As each person takes their own personal power into their hands to begin this journey, so do they bring to their selves the success that will be theirs. This journey is one that moves into self, not anywhere else but back to self, to the health and wellness of the daily self and the Higher Self. The ability to make the journey from what is to what can be, to move beyond a current life of dis-ease and claim the intended life of wellness – this is the transformation awaiting to be experienced.

Personal Power Seeds for Wellness

- I value my self highly and choose to maintain my physical and emotional self in alignment and optimal health.
- I give thanks for the wellness and abundance in my life now.
- I visualize and feel my Soul and its healing.
- I emerge now, as a butterfly from the cocoon, into the sunshine of my renewed life.
- All is well with my Soul.
- I have been released to move forward in wellness.
- Those past life traumas hold no power over me today.

We have control over the trajectory of our lives. If someone else has control, it is because we have given that control away, thereby giving over our power to another. That is not a good thing and usually results in unhappiness and unfulfillment. This is the truth of this life. We wish to speak of this in order to bring trust back to each person: trust in their selves that they can travel the road intended for them and wished for by them. All is doable if they allow it.

We are enabled to find the trust in our selves needed to make the change in this life by making needed changes in our past lives. There is a clear path to finding success by following the steps as they are set out.

We address those whose lives are difficult now and encourage them to consider this process and enter into the trust in their selves required to undertake the journey.

*What we believe we are and can
be becomes who we are.*

Do all people know this truth? Perhaps not, and it is our role now to cast light on these realities. We are certain that the link to the past is felt by those reading these words. When that feeling is understood and accepted, the steps toward healing may begin.

What each person can absorb by understanding their past life connections is personal to them. For each person, there will be a different threshold of acceptance and willingness to jump into this process and find their way to wellness. But what is to come is worth the jump, or as some would describe it, "a leap of faith."

We say now that the leap of faith is faith in one's self. Each person must take that leap, based on their own belief that their Higher Self is always present to guide and protect.

The key to each person's success is their belief in their selves — each person has the ability to trust in their selves, and if they do then nothing is impossible for them in this or any future lifetime. It is guaranteed.
~Pax

Pax reminds us: there will be no harm, there will be no failed attempts once the whole self is engaged in the intention to take this step to the next level of wellness.

Do they, that former you and your Higher Self, wish for your highest and best good now in this life? Yes is the answer, and this Soul Healing process is the path to that wellness.

We have shared much with your world on topics unrelated to the Soul Healing process, but always based on the premise that the health of your people was good and sufficient to support the journey forward. Now we see that those wishing to help save your Planet Mother Earth are often in need of saving their selves. We wish to bring healing forward and to all your people in need of help finding their way.

It is our joy to witness the healing experienced by those who manage to meld their past and their present into a unified, healthy persona. Having healed their souls, they are well enough, emotionally, and physically, to undertake the next chapter in their life. Taking strengths, gifts, and abilities from past lifetimes and merging them with today's ambitions is another gift of this process – it is not entirely about healing past harms and includes recognition of strengths. Going forward in trust is the key, as is knowing the ability to flourish in this world is equaled by the ability to teach and share what has been a blessing to learn and put into effect in this life.

This is the joy that comes from wholeness and wellness and optimism combined. Now we look toward the future, when the majority of your people enjoy all these attributes, bringing peace and harmony to your world.

Your Personal Archive of Lives to Access

This ability of past lifetimes to control, in some ways, the present lifetime – this reminds us that Soul Wisdom is complete and integral. It combines all that is with all that was.

Consider that the experience from all past lifetimes is condensed into the present moment of your Soul. It is an amazing thought, one that can be hard for some to understand and to accept. Yet others have an immediate recognition of this as fact.

> *Think of it, each person, this is your Akashic Record, stored within your Self and available for you to access.*

Do you feel it? Do you know the power of this ability? Imagine having a library available to you, one that contains details of everything that ever took place in your world. It is there for you to access – your own archive of lives to learn from and to grow from. Imagine!

How would you use this wisdom and guidance? The question is important, because that is what is available to you now, to help you navigate your world today. Unlimited is the guidance found within this library, which is housed within your Soul. Its knowledge is not available to anyone else and completely dedicated to the betterment of you and your current life. This is what is offered to you now, in this book of guidance.

> *Soul Healing is the method and the process for you to unleash this energy of wellness, growth, and healing for your highest and best use.*

You may access your historical records, your personal Akashic Records as readily as you visit personal past lifetimes. The processes of connecting with your Higher Self, with your Guides, to accompany and direct you on this journey begins with the same first step. The destination is different, however, and your request for an overview, or a close-up view of what came before, is your choice. Each can be visited in depth or viewed simply as an awareness of your existence in those past places in time.

While Akashic Records are a collection of all Universal events, your personal history throughout lifetimes is within you, within your Soul Memory for you to access as your personal library. This place of learning everything about your past, present, and future is yours to view – an amazing thought and an accessible reality.

Peace in your heart is your destiny and your right, and through this awareness comes the clarity for your steps into the past, your past. Take all you can from the highs and lows of your lifetimes and learn from them. Being open to receive, this is the mindset needed to step forward in this adventure. The guidance of your Higher Self means this journey is protected as you are protected along the way. Witnessing what was and what will be is an extraordinary experience. Know that you need only be present in the moment to benefit from this gift. Trust in your self to accept healing and in your Higher Self to serve as Guide.

When we speak of following your heart, as we often do, it means for you to feel your inner voice and hear its message. For it is this rather than intellectual thinking that leads you, based on the wisdom of your personal library. This is the trajectory of your healing, if that is what you seek, and your Journey to Wellness in all forms.

Our guidance is there for the taking, we say, and we wish to illuminate the process for you by directing you to your own inner guides. You know you have guidance, do you not? Each person who goes within will find their companions are already with them in wisdom and tolerance and patience. You may call this what you wish: intuition, sixth sense, that little voice within – it is all the same. The important piece is that you feel it, hear it, and listen. Guidance is there, accompanied by love and the intention for you to succeed and find wellness.

When it becomes comfortable and familiar to be aware of your inner wisdom, in whatever manner it is presented, the ability to hear and feel guidance and respond to it grows.

Have you considered that many of your past lifetimes may have been lived as important, wise, and influential people? The integrity and knowledge of your past remains within you and colors your ways of today. You may sometimes wonder why you think or do what seems to originate from someone else. In many cases, it is indeed a someone else that guides your hand; but still that someone else was you in another time. Is this hard to imagine? Harder still to believe? Spend some time considering the possibility, and you will find a cosmic logic at work in the concept of inner wisdom and guidance being yours for the taking.

As a complex and individual person, you are made up of many interwoven parts, partly because of your history, which remains in your DNA. Is there a way to see it, to visualize strands of DNA that can be attributed to past lifetime identities? One day, this vision will be a reality. The maze of personal identities will be subjected to deep scrutiny.

At this point in time, we trust in that destiny and go forward in the Knowingness of it.

> *Each person knows what they feel, and each*
> *person feels what they know. ~Pax*

Moving ahead in time, there will be other advances that bring your people closer to attunement with their past lifetime identities and the links they have to present day selves. This is the point of knowing, yes? It is to be a source of healing, a source of wellness, and a source of strength for each person to access as they choose. Knowing this resource is available to each person is a blessing, and the ability to access and utilize that wisdom is a gift.

The Wind Beneath Your Wings

Having this wind beneath your wings is as the wind beneath angel wings – an inner strength recognized as yours to take and use in joy and wellness, growth and wisdom. Trust and believe in your self as well as your Higher Self to protect and guide. Soul Healing is a roadmap to growth of your own inner wisdom and vision, available to all and accepted by seekers who find the way to self-knowledge through this journey.

The journey within, to access the Higher Self, is how we have described the Soul Healing process outlined in this book. There are reasons to communicate with one's Higher Self that range from curiosity to healing, from seeking validation to asking for moral support during a trying time. The journey of life need not be undertake alone. The blessing of knowing and accepting the presence of your angels, your spirit guides, your inner wisdom, intuition, or that little voice within – whatever you may choose to call the presence – is that you are empowered and protected. You can avail your self of the guidance that is received whenever you ask. Yes, it is good to ask for what you want in all areas of life, and this is one.

Moving forward and away from a current day dependency habit is virtually impossible without understanding the source connection and history.

Breaking the chain linking to a time that did not serve you well – this is a healing pathway to wellness.

> *Your Journey to Wellness is found by*
> *going within – no passport required.*
> *~Pax*

Addictions Understood – Personal Journeys

We now focus on addictions, substance abuse, and other wellness challenges. Whether the substance in question is tobacco, alcohol, or drugs, or not a substance at all but an activity, the pain of dependence is equivalent and real.

Shared here, in the following pages, are several personal Journeys to Wellness: some more lengthy, some less so. They are shared by people who have been offered alternatives to finding their own healing, through means that do not involve reliance on medication to diffuse symptoms or buffer against the reality of who they are.

Alcohol Dependency

Having come to the understanding that alcohol had been her friend and her crutch in a past lifetime, she undertook to relieve that friend (alcohol) of the need to visit her daily, now.

We speak of a person who had not severed the ties to a past lifetime, when there was much substance abuse, particularly of alcohol. She tells of the need to numb her senses and dull down her awareness of personal issues she could not control. Rather, they controlled her. There were people in her life who used and abused her. She found no ability to manage or escape their control, either. Alcohol use got her through her life; it came to be a friend to her – a crutch and a constant companion. She relied on this dulling of the senses to allow her to get through each day. Thus, the habit formed. To think of approaching her daily life with clear head and acute senses – this was not within her ability at that time, in that past life, and she descended deeper and deeper into the pit of losing her self.

As that lifetime ended and she left it behind, her Soul Memory held the impression of how alcohol had become her constant companion and friend in need. When she was re-introduced to it in her current lifetime, there was a connection, a familiarity, and a comfort she did not question. As time went on, she grew into the habit of medicating her self, without consciousness of the reason, which was self-preservation. The feeling of comfort grew, while the awareness of her surroundings and pain lessened. She became dependent on the harmful habit. She did not question the choice to drink, denied her dependency. Such is the way of a substance abuser.

Do we say this was not her fault? Perhaps. Do we say she was unaware of the reasons she felt magnetized to alcohol? Indeed. She had not considered a past life habit as the source of her present lifetime's dependency, that one was responsible for the other, but it is so. Her Soul Memory carries the threads, carries the dregs from her past forward to today. Once considered, the power of past life influence is undeniable. Remaining connected, one to the other without understanding – this is to continue the harmful habits we inherit from our selves. There must be awareness in order to break that link in the long chain of dependence.

When the day came to introduce this person to her past and allow the film of past lifetimes to play, she immediately recognized the beginning of her relationship with alcohol. She saw that she was – then and now – a victim of her oppressors from the past, a victim of her dependency on alcohol, which transcended lifetimes. The light dawned on her. She saw the connection clearly, she felt the connection, and better still she was able to recognize that she could release her use of alcohol, knowing it need serve no further purpose for her in this life. This was an epiphany, a grand awareness and releasing of that part of her past she had been unaware of that nonetheless controlled her present life.

When she entered the Soul Healing process and became acquainted with the woman she was in that most difficult past lifetime, she felt empathy for her and found that this experience brought her to kindness, understanding, and compassion. As she repeated her past life visits through the Soul Healing process, she extended these feelings to additional past selves she met and vowed to learn more of her history. This led to a more empathetic nature developing in her present life.

Knowing one's background and history allows for deeper understanding of the person of today. What motivations, what triggers, what strengths, and what challenges have come forward to present time? All can be addressed, all can be healed, all can be learned from. These are all compelling reasons for taking the Journey to Wellness through Soul Healing.

Having come to the understanding that alcohol had been her friend and her crutch in that past lifetime, she undertook to relieve that friend from the need to visit her daily. It was an awareness and a release. As with many friends, alcohol could be enjoyed occasionally but with no need for perpetual closeness.

She lives today in fulfillment and happiness, with gratitude for her successful journey and trust in her present self. She trusts that her Higher Self will be her companion in finding what her future brings. Her vision for her self is a trigger-free life of joy and contributing to the wellness of others as best she can through sharing her own journey. Her belief now in her self has grown to the extent that she considers her reclaimed personal power to be her greatest gift. Fortunately for her, physical health has remained strong. Emotional wellness grew along with her newfound belief in her self. Her vision of life now is one of positivity and peace in her heart.

Addictions fade in the light of your personal power

Drug Abuse

He decided he no longer wanted to be that person the drugs created.

It is a sadness for the world when a person who has been productive and happy becomes pushed to risk life and wellness through drug use, drug abuse, and abdication of responsibility for health, career, and family relationships. Has this become common in your world of today? We say it is so. Further, we must question the basis for a decision to leave a stable place in life and go over the edge of reasoning in this way. It is the pull of history – that which triggers the present self and renders one incapable of reasoning or wise decision making. When someone is constantly triggered, they undergo a personality change: one that prepares them for fight or flight at any moment. This anxious state contributes further to their depth of unwellness and dis-ease.

Our next subject for discussion was a man who had much to lose. He saw his own self as stuck in a place not of his making. So breaking out to a place that was of his own making was chosen as the path forward. What happens to a person when the stimulation of an altered reality becomes greater than the reality of their daily life? In this case, he chose to be someone other than who he presented to his world. Who was that person?

It was his own self of another time in history, another lifetime, with another personality entirely – one who was unstable, who was a reckless adventurer unconcerned with the need to follow established practices or embrace responsibility; who took advantage of all in his path. Living as that person and personality from a past time and society, he was ruthless in his treatment of all around him. Eventually, he gained control over many. Continuing to seek higher ambitions and greater thrills led him to experiment with hallucinogenics – albeit those found in nature. With the increasing use of mind-altering substances, he became more of a tyrant and was responsible for the demise of many. As he dove deeper into living in constantly altered states of consciousness, he became less aware of the damage he was responsible for. When responsibility did enter his mind, more drugs were used to blunt the reality of his destructive actions.

The person he is today has flashbacks of that past lifetime in his thoughts, feelings, and an inner knowing that there is a dark history he has not explored. As the picture continues to darken, so does the need to block it out. The choice of using drugs to numb the mind becomes a self-fulfilling prophesy – history repeating itself. The darkness grows and instills fear and unwillingness to uncover the truth of what is gnawing at the conscious mind. So, denial and self-destruction continues.

This is where we began the journey to visit pertinent past lifetimes and link today's pull toward drug use with the power drugs held over him in past. Recognizing those experiences, understanding, and releasing: his Journey to Wellness began with the recognition that there is a direct link that can be released, so that healing may begin.

In the case of this man, he faced a long road ahead. There was denial of the need combined with unwillingness to completely leave drugs behind. This was based on the enjoyment drugs brought to him as well as his lack of personal power. When sufficient time was given to reflect on who he had become in this present life, it came clear to him that the personality he had developed was responsible for his loss of family, friends, career, home, self-respect, and good health and wellness, both physical and emotional.

The picture was bleak. A great deal of mental preparation took place before he entered the Soul Healing process. When he did, there was a reluctance, at first, to absorb what he saw and felt. But the reality of it was undeniable. As he approached these visits to his past lifetime with an open mind and heart, he was impacted greatly and ultimately ready to have a dialog with that person he had once been – ready to understand the connection, the link between then and his current self, and truly open to understanding why he was drawn to drugs now. More importantly, he decided what his intention was, going forward, regarding drug use.

There was hesitation to commit to abstaining. He thought he could use drugs sparingly. Then, over time and through more dialog with this past life personae, there came a realization that he could release this dependence completely. He decided he no longer wanted to be that person the drugs created, that for better or worse the person he was now, without drugs, would be the personality he would build upon for his future. This took time. He allowed the time and grew into the person he wanted to be, drug-free and somewhat chagrined that he had taken the present life path he had. His clarity of vision without drugs allowed him to strengthen mind and body and rebuild life in his own, intentional way. It was a successful journey for him, and he remains healthy and well today.

He has chosen to lead a quiet life. As he rebuilds his self-esteem, one step at a time, he enjoys his newfound freedom from the influence of a substance that created within him a persona he now felt ashamed of. Those days are gone, he now says. The future is what he will make of it. This knowing that he has complete control over who he is, and his vision of who he will be, brings him freedom and personal pride.

He has gone on to write about his experiences while living his quiet life, thus enabling him to satisfy his need to teach, lead by example, and keep the low profile he cherishes.

People are not addicted to drugs; they are addicted to escaping reality.

A Need for Gambling

She undertook the stages of personal healing with peace and trust that she was being guided and protected, emerging into the light of her new awareness with relief and gratitude. Returning wellness to others is her focus now.

What can account for the need to take chances with life, limb, and finances to the extent that all can be lost? While the average person does not encounter this level of risk in daily life, there is a large segment of the population that is unable to control their need to wager some or all the money or possessions they have on the prospect of winning more. This becomes an overwhelming need to plan for the next big windfall. What is not considered is the potential for a next big loss, and herein lies the problem. While it is sometimes good to view life through rose-colored glasses, it is unwise to block out reality. Too many lives have been hurt, irreparably damaged, or even lost as a result of exchanging reality for blind hope. It is always good to hope, but in some forms hope can be twisted into an irrational need to ignore our responsibilities.

Money for one's rent or mortgage is sometimes hard to accumulate, each and every month. For this woman with a gambling addiction, that was the case. Why then would she risk losing what little she had? Could she win more money than she needed, thus adding value to her life? That value would have been food and warmth and the comforts she lacked, so the risks seemed an acceptable gamble to take. This is what she thought too often, and it took her down a path to fear and failure, personal harm and ultimately living on the streets. She was an innocent by nature and felt she would prevail every time she wagered her meagre amount of money trying for more. Why?

As we searched the pattern of her past lifetimes, we found her in a similar situation in her present life. At one time, she was connected to people who used her and essentially trained her to believe in luck, to believe that luck was her friend and would always be on her side. It was not to be. In time, she became addicted to the prospect of winning and more deeply descended into the abyss of losing. She became immersed in the culture of gambling to the extent that she lost friends and family and, ultimately, her wellness. Living out her days in servitude as a result, she continued to gamble on anything she could. She craved the visceral reaction of anticipation, wins, and losses. Her total commitment to possibility drove her in all ways. This powerful Soul Memory remained and continued to call to her for fulfillment. It demanded a sense of being enveloped by and permeated with the feeling of winning.

On the edge of total deterioration and disappearance into the shadows, she felt agreeable to investigating what was controlling her now, and why.

She had had no thoughts of past lifetimes being relevant to her today, or that they existed at all. But through intercessions by others who knew the truth, she was finally rescued.

It was a long road taken by those who believed in her, and they did so to the extent that she was given care and shelter and counselling. Open, non-judgmental care from supporters allowed for conversations to turn to the possibility of looking outside her current situation to understand triggers and find the source of her inability to control this addiction.

She showed remarkable strength in focusing on working through the Soul Healing process and absorbing what her past showed her. This included the strong pull, even then, to try acquiring more than she had by any means possible. There was revealed to her a history of stealing and betting and falsifying what was in order to gain more. She did not like what she saw or felt about who she was and what she had done. She found her past distasteful and felt embarrassed by it.

Witnessing the compulsion in her past self brought powerful feelings forward, along with the realization that she could overcome what was and create what will be: good emotional strength and health. Leaving gambling behind, releasing the control it once had, and replacing it with gratitude for regained freedom and wellness led to renewed life and happiness. This was not an easy or fast process for her, but the strength of her intention to find wellness supported her through her Journey to Wellness. She undertook the stages of personal healing with peace and trust that she was being guided and protected – and she emerged into the light of her new awareness with relief and gratitude.

Knowing that something from so long ago, that was so powerful in that lifetime, will have no further power today diffused the triggers. She has since committed to counselling others in need of reclaiming their personal power, particularly over addictions. She has stepped into her true purpose in this lifetime, which is helping others with addictions find clarity, understanding, release, and personal healing and peace. Returning wellness to others is her focus now.

Co-Dependence: Healing the Broken Spirit

She gained the power of her own convictions and became self-sufficient and trusting in her own choices and abilities. These attributes she showed to others and taught by example.

There is much to be said for self-confidence, empowerment, and a strong personal nature. These positive traits usually reflect trust in self. Little do most people know that it is as important to have trust in your Higher Self, the inner voice and feeling you sometimes are aware of but may dismiss. This is your Soul Memory alerting you, guiding you, protecting you with an intuitive knowing of how to proceed with people, places, and experiences, if you will open to receiving.

There are those on their Path to Wellness now who came into this world without strong self-confidence, or sometimes none at all. We speak with these individuals to learn what triggers this need to place trust outside of their selves, in other people to guide them through life, while never questioning what they are told. This extends to relationships with teachers, employers, professionals of all kinds, friends, family, or even acquaintances. Anyone who will give an opinion will be heard and favored in place of forming a personal opinion or intention. Sound familiar?

This reliance on others can be connected to past lifetimes, when that person was not permitted to think for their self, or if they did punishment was the response. Being submissive to parents or partners or both, became a constant and limiting state of being, while deviating from it brought negative repercussions.

Is it the case that today those emotional remnants, those expectations of punishment remain strong in the subconscious? These Soul Memories, or Cell Memories as they are also known, are powerful and result in an inner expectation that showing initiative and having an opinion can bring pain and punishment. How can a person change this in their present without understanding that they will not be hurt? Just as importantly, what is the root cause of these warning flashes and the inability to want to direct their own life?

Before resolution can be found, there must be a combination of healing modalities that involve awareness of what transpired when they lived in another time and place in history, of how and why they were treated as they were and by whom. By knowing the ability to forgive those involved and release them from any connection to present day life, we can release lingering influences that result in a current inability to take personal responsibility for our life choices.

Just as important is the need to reclaim personal power and move ahead in life, trusting in self and Higher Self. It is in the knowing and belief that self-empowerment is a good and beneficial part of a healthy individual's make-up that personal power can be accepted and claimed as a right.

It so often is women who, throughout history, have been subjugated to the male dominance of their world. That dominance has left scars still visible today.

These scars were seen when we met a woman whose fear of taking charge, taking control, or even speaking her opinions left her helpless and unable to function in a useful way in business. Even her personal life became complicated, as she constantly looked outside of her own self for answers, for guidance, and for making decisions. It had reached a point where she felt unwilling to leave her house each day for fear she would need to make choices at her job and someone would be displeased. This was crippling her lifestyle and ability to function.

When she learned of the Soul Healing process, she was excited to think there may be help for her and decided to participate. This was the first of many good decisions she made for her self beginning that day.

As she regressed back to the most recent lifetime, where her memory triggers originated, it was clear that her oppression of that time was severe and accompanied by punishment, pain, shame, and eventual guilt with all that entailed. It was a time of females being little more than invisible servants who were not to be heard or considered equal to or even worthy of notice by the males who controlled them.

She had a strong will, initially, and opinions about the treatment of her self and other women in her situation. As she repeatedly tried to find ways to bring equality to treatment of women in her situation, she incurred the wrath of her "keepers" and others who witnessed her behavior. Over time, she continued to be punished, ever more harshly. As they were guilty by association with her, so were the women she tried to help.

Her spirit was ultimately broken, and she ceased her opposition in order to protect others damaged as a result of her efforts to help. There was no justice – only pain, guilt, and a resolve to remain quiet from then on.

Recognizing this past experience through the Soul Healing process and the particular journey she undertook was an epiphany for her: a wide-screen view of her declared guilt and shrinking away from speaking her thoughts and opinions. Knowing the extent of her victimization in that past life, and the strength she once had, this changed how she would remember the self she was then. She felt proud of her self of that time for trying to make a positive difference, for only giving up her cause when it was clear she may not live through further punishment.

This viewing of her past, coupled with a resulting surge in her self-esteem and pride in how much she had tried to be a change-maker, this resulted in her taking up, once more, the cause of bringing equality and justice to women of today, those who do not have tools to make change for their selves.

She extended her work to include children in schools who had little in the way of resources at home as well as a lack of self-esteem and personal power. The difference she made in their lives and education was remarkable. Her dedication to service extended to continued growth in her own life and self-worth. She gained the power of her own convictions and became self-sufficient and trusting in her own choices and abilities. These attributes she showed others and taught by example.

That she went on to receive recognition and awards for her innovative work with children was a validation and a gift for her. Many accolades came her way, and her life was dominated by continuing to expand her philosophies and practices to reach more children – and by extension their parents. Going on to create wellness within family units resulted in a boost for those seeking education and a higher level of achievement among her learning groups.

Becoming aware and enabled to choose to release that hold the past has on the present is empowering.

Depression in Men of Today

Why is it that the progression in linear time does not equate with progression in intelligence or wellness in your people?

Why is there so much looking outward to ensure personal safety? Why is external protection sought to ensure that personal space remains personal and property is protected? Is your world now one where living in fear of others has become the norm? If these questions provoke affirmative answers, then it is a sorry state you find your selves in. What to do?

There are those who take control of their lives and manage these fears, or better still alleviate these fears. But for those whose lives are impacted negatively, the resultant feelings of inadequacy can lead to a potential for depression. Here we have the spinning years, or possibly lifetimes, riddled with inability to take control. How is it that this has become prevalent in your present time? What has led to the preponderance of unfulfilled and unhappy males of your species?

We say there is no shortage of explanations for this, from recent generations of little boys who did not learn from their elders how to be strong; how to acquire life skills and use them; or how to understand that not everyone wins or passes grades or moves up. They did not learn that failure is something to learn from, that not everyone will be picked for the team. This stays in the psyche.

Taken as a whole, each person has many gifts and talents, but it seems that nobody is questioned about their abilities as a youngster. It is the way, instead, to praise and pass and allow forward motion even where it has not been earned. This conditioning instills a false sense of security and does not prepare young people for the realities of adult life in the big world. Witness the many men who fall apart if not chosen for a job or a school or a team or a relationship. Automatically labeling these events as failures is far from what should be considered correct and real in your time and place. It is not a wonder, therefore, that depression abounds in your world.

How can you approach the need to reveal that inadequacy is not in the person, but rather in the manner in which the person was treated while growing up? A false sense of security, once given, is difficult to understand and put aside in favor of the realities of life. A new, healthful philosophy of living is hard to adopt, harder to understand and accept, and almost impossible to live by – because it means taking responsibility for one's self in all ways. Coming up and out of a protected lifestyle is confusing and demeaning and debilitating for many. Yours is considered a cruel and unjust world thereafter, not one into which a person willingly enters and participates.

When the day comes when a person recognizes that a new time is upon them, there will be anger and disbelief as well as grief for what in their past lifestyle is gone forever. Mixed and powerful emotions lead to a feeling of despair. How to survive is the question.

What is lost is the belief that someone else will always be there to rescue us. This expectation should be exchanged for the reality of being on one's own to survive and thrive. There is no external rescue now, as there is inner guidance – complete rescue from within. Personal power has been reclaimed.

What is needed to effect this form of self-rescue? It is inner strength, trust in self, personal power. These are all within and, when sourced, when asked for, emerge in strength to guide and protect. Men have been conditioned since they were little boys that they are to be strong, however there are many whose strength did not become fulfilled, as others always led the way for them. Now that the tables have turned, and the same men are expected to lead, only fear rises to meet the challenge, not strength.

Now we ask whether past lives are related to this fear, or if they originate with the current lifetime. The most recent is a result of the most distant that has not been healed, and by this we refer to past lifetimes that remain connected to the present, though the strong cord of memory. This cord exists, and it is wound from Soul Memories, or as some would think them Cell Memories. It is that powerful. Soul Memory is a life-controlling and life-altering reality. Do not dismiss this truth as unimportant or unrelated to present challenges.

How to apply the Soul Healing process to finding present day wellness? Visits to past lifetimes are the beginning of the Journey to Wellness. To anticipate finding a relevant set of experiences in a past lifetime should not be the only intention, rather, being open to what will be found: there is the way. Trusting begins with small steps, and that means being open to what will come. This, for those unaccustomed to standing on their own, can be frightening.

Trusting in the Higher Self to protect us and trusting in the present self to accept what is felt, what is seen or heard – this is the partnership that will bring progress along the Journey to Wellness. There is no shame involved for a man recognizing that he lacks in personal emotional wellness, personal power, or the ability to takes steps outside of his comfort zone. This is growing and changing and adding to personal wellness through acceptance of his deservedness. Knowing and believing that personal strength and wellness are his birthright brings him the confidence needed to step into the process with joy.

Feeling gratification, freedom, and love for self throughout this process only grows as wellness returns. We say returns, as somewhere and at some time in the Soul's journey there was wholeness and wellness. Now, as it is reclaimed, there is celebration within the Soul family and recognition that life going forward will grow healthy. Trust in Self and self will be restored.

You may say it is the best of both worlds. We may say it is the best of all worlds, as they collide and create.

A Woman's Depression

As she entered the next phase of her life in wellness, her contributions to childhood education became her reason for being.

In this world, we detect a serious inability to recognize wellness as a deserved state of being for all people. That was certainly the case for this person who we met on her journey to find answers. When she recognized that she had many previous lifetimes, the most recent being one of great responsibility for many people, particularly children, it opened her to remembering who she was and more than one incident where she could not protect others. Failure to protect children, this was a great sadness that she felt deep within her self in her present lifetime but did not know why. The depth of sadness she carried within grew as she went through life. It colored her choices and actions. She spiraled down into personal failure, at least in her own mind.

When a person feels at a loss to understand their emotions, yet feels they are a failure, it brings significant change to their way of life. It hinders their willingness to remain a part of society and their ability to look upon their selves with love. Next there is a spiral downward into a place where self-love and respect are replaced with self-loathing and need to disassociate from the present self. Here is where this woman found her self, without knowing why. But she openly speaks of depression as a constant presence.

As she became aware of the cloud of this past lifetime and experiences over her present, she was motivated to learn who she was when she lived before, and what the circumstances were that left her Soul Memory as deeply impacted as she felt it to be. The Soul Healing process presented a pathway to healing and the ability to release her present self from the grip of a past life's guilt.

Learning that her inability to protect others at that time was not within her control – and that she her self was victimized – this allowed her release of the emotions controlling her present as well as the inability to rise to the awareness that she can claim happiness and wellness, each deserved in her present lifetime.

Time passed while she made more than one visit to that past lifetime to fully understand her role there, to recognize the inequality that existed with resulting lack of control over her life. She was ultimately able to forgive her self and those responsible, to release the feelings and visions of that past time. By understanding this previously unknown and powerful influence over her present, she became able to let go of the sadness surrounding her and gradually realize she was innocent of the perceived wrongdoing by her past self. It was out of her control. While her heart felt she had failed, her head now told her that was not the case. Reconciling these competing thoughts and feelings was a part of her Journey to Wellness. She found balance in her past and her present selves, then grew from the experience of knowing both much better.

As she entered the next phase of her life in wellness, her contributions to childhood education became her reason for being. The impact her teachings, her love, and her caring had on children with little family support, this became a turning point for many of them. Her legacy was one of great caring for the lives of many people. In time, her work became a model for others to follow.

A Man's Anxiety

Now he has taken back his power over past as well as present, and as a result his future is one he will manage well.

When this man approached his out-of-control emotions in such a way that he attempted to find cause and resolution, he became open to exploring the possibility that the source of anxiety was not found in his current world. When he could not find a link, he became a seeker of more esoteric means of locating his Path to Wellness. It takes curiosity and it takes trust to make this choice and act on it. In his case, there was also trust in self that he would be protected in this journey – and so he was.

As he spoke of anxiety ruling his life and not understanding why, he also spoke of people he knew and experiences they had relating to their own anxieties. It seems he surrounded his own self with people who lived daily with their own anxieties, did not seek understanding of why, but came together as a group to share stories and feelings. That sharing ultimately resulted in deepening the level of anxiety for all involved. They all reveled in the belief that their lives were normal, that debilitating anxiety was normal, and their support group was useful only in validating these beliefs – misguided as they were.

He began to reveal thoughts that made little sense to him, as they were unrelated to his current life experiences. It became clear that Soul Memories from a past life were intruding, were pushing through to the surface of his awareness, causing him fear and despair over the inability to manage or rid his own self of these unfamiliar thoughts.

As he came to recognize that his anxious thoughts and mental pictures were originating from a past lifetime, and as he was enabled to view that life as an observer, he recognized the link between his life then and his present anxiety. There was no clear connection in lifestyles, between his past and present selves, but there remained a deep need to release what was a very real situation of that past time influencing his daily activities in the present. His inability to complete a need he felt strongly about – this left him unable to clear his subconscious and move ahead in wellness in his present life.

This man brought his heightened state of anxiety to everything he did, including the Soul Healing process. Over time and repeated attempts to quiet his mind sufficiently to trust in self and connect with his past, he saw that he was able to become focused on this task, this vision he had set for his own self of a quiet and peaceful conversation with whomever he was going to find among his past selves. He treated this process as a great adventure, which for him it was. He was not disappointed.

This journey revealed at least one past lifetime where each day broke with the prospect of not living through it. While it was a time of kill or be killed, hunt or be hunted, it was not-so-long ago in linear time for him as in his personal evolution through lifetimes. A thread of powerful memory and feeling existed that brought almost visceral reactions to him without an understanding of why. This is a life-altering and threatening experience for a person who has no knowledge of its origin.

As he began the journey into his past, he opened to newfound clarity, along with the opportunity to dialog with his past selves. This became the basis of his self-healing: this opening to awareness and acceptance and the knowing that his present day emotions were based on past facts, albeit generated from a time he had known nothing about.

This man changed his life completely, when he came to terms with the level of safety and security he had in his present life. He recognized the need to express daily gratitude for the life he currently had, and he was to continue growing as a person as a next step on his path forward. His life became one of giving and sharing and teaching, a role he willingly accepted.

The relief that he felt in knowing what caused his anxiety, and the change in his ability to function in a healthy way, this brought remarkable improvement, empowerment, and wellness to his life. He was able to move forward in happiness, in trust for his ability to manage all that came his way, freed from any questioning of this new reality.

Were there ever times when a feeling of anxiety slipped into his consciousness? Yes, briefly. But he now had the tools needed to manage those thoughts and neutralize them as they entered his mind. He is able to recognize and understand the previous connection and diffuse his trigger reactions. Now he has taken back his power over past as well as present. As a result, his future is one he will manage well.

Trauma Comes Back as a Reaction, not a Memory.

Liberation: Living Your New Story

Uncontrollable Anger, Rage

Soul Healing: this is his gift to him self now, and to all in his circle who support him on this journey forward and away from his pain and anger, toward newfound understanding of self and the world around him.

We speak now about uncontrollable emotion, which ranges from uncomfortable to damaging to life-threatening for self and others.

This lack of emotional control is all-too common and comes with pain and hurt, fear and trauma, indignity, and the inability to comprehend why no good comes to the suffering person, only negativity and harm, real and perceived. There is no trust that a change in attitude will bring a change in what comes to him. Such was the case, for this man who brought forward his need to "diffuse his life", so he said. He meant to remove the anger from his mind and body, as he feared his lack of control at times.

Past lives may or may not have been greatly harmful to this person, or they may have been slightly harmful. But the result is a heightened expectation that around every corner is potential harm that is intended for no reason but to hurt him. This belief, we find, escalates over time, and anger toward people extends to anger toward places and things as well as those in power, those in control and command, and complete belief that it is only a matter of time until they all escalate their attack on him. This belief is based on lack of trust that there is any good feeling toward him, and only trust that hate is what is directed toward him. It is an irrational belief based on nothing he could identify, but it affected all aspects of his current life.

Anger builds. There is no perception of why this is, just a knowing that everyone is out to hurt and discredit and make life impossible for him. He believes he is innocent of any wrongdoing. This internal and unmanageable belief grows and intensifies to the boiling point of rage, which can result in harm to self and others.

Helping this person to visit the past lifetimes responsible for his current anger was life-altering for him. The Soul Healing process created awareness of what was done to him in the past, and what he participated in, that has culminated in this at-times uncontrollable and damaging anger.

Many lifetimes spent as a man who was misguided and filled with insecurities established a negative pattern deep within him. There became a need to seek approval from others. When it was not given, there was anger because he felt approval was deserved. Over the course of his lifetimes that repeated unhelpful mindsets and traumatic experiences, he replaced the need for approval with belief there would be none. Therefore, anger replaced the previous approval seeking. Just anger at the beginning. Then, instead of communicating, he would isolate and react badly when there the approval he expected was not forthcoming.

It was a decreasing circle he functioned within, until it became apparent there would be no connection with others and no healthy functioning within family, social, or work circles. There was a need to live as a single entity who needed no one. This grew to declining friendships and personal connections. Resentment grew into anger, and the belief that he was being punished and ostracized soon followed. These feelings deepened and were accompanied by growing distrust and anger, one lifetime after another. It became self-fulfilling and deeply damaging to his mental and emotional wellbeing. As a result, his physical health deteriorated, and his overall decline could not be halted by traditional means. Even psychological intervention was not successful, because he did not support the process to the extent needed and refused to accept that any negative behaviors or challenges were within his control.

The many previous lives this man had lived, which deepened his belief that he was a victim of hate and injustice, had essentially cemented these feelings within him. In his current manifestation and in his Soul Memories, he carried the fear of being alone in the world, a victim without the tools to improve his situation.

Beginning to visit his past lifetimes, in order to see that his fear and anger were largely self-inflicted, was an awakening for him. Soon, he wanted to explore more and more, to go deeper and deeper. This became life-altering for him, and although it was profound it was not quick. He required much time and patience to truly see and feel who he had been and how those more damaging lifetimes evolved into who he was now. He took responsibility for his actions and claimed responsibility for what was his contribution to the dysfunction of those past personas.

It was therapeutic to recognize the source, the root cause. Afterward, there could begin an understanding that would enable him to recognize that he is not always under attack and does not need to look at those around him as potential aggressors. To recognize he has allies and is not a target, this was a breakthrough in relaxing his previous defensiveness and learning to release fear and anger.

Because of his determination and openness in the Soul Healing process, he came to understand those past lives for what they were and disconnect them from his present. He released the chain binding him to the influence of those past times and the traumatic experiences that did not serve his wellbeing.

This is his gift to him self, now, and to all in his circle who support him on this journey forward and away from his pain and anger, toward newfound understanding of him self and the world around him.

Racism, Intolerance, Superiority

In time, he shifted his beliefs and trigger responses and relaxed into a more open and accepting personality.

This man's story centers on his perceived racial superiority and belief that it is justified in reality. There are deep-seated reasons for these beliefs that include his conditioning of time and place as well as past life experiences, although those lifetimes' racial hatreds were the result of conditioning as well.

Throughout history, genocides were supported by those believing in their own superiority and that another race or religion had no place in their country, or world. Superiority and exclusionary views led some to feel that other groups did not deserve to live. The long story of the human species is filled with atrocities that had no basis in humanity, only a basis in hatred and self-deluded superiority of those oppressors who took their beliefs to the militant population, who in turn set out to annihilate entire races and religions of innocent people.

Those involved in these violent actions come into successive lifetimes still holding hatred and a need to diminish or end the lives and cultures of those they consider inferior. It is a dangerous festering of a need to harm others. It grows beyond any hope of containment in certain periods. In other times, it lurks beneath the surface of many people going about their ordinary, daily lives.

In our regression sessions with this man, he was guided to the source of his present intolerance of others who do not look like him. He was led to learn of his inhumane behaviors of past times. Like for others with hate instilled in them as children, his tendencies grew as he developed a full-grown need to hate and harm. Unchecked hatred that grows from one lifetime to another, that is the course we offer a path to terminating.

> *Removal of hatred from a person's heart is life-altering for them, healing, and transformational.*

A long-standing belief in personal and racial superiority had led this man to a lifetime of unhappiness. As he went through life showing disrespect and intolerance for those he deemed unworthy and less-than, his ability to maintain work, family, and relationships was lessened. Deepening arrogance and impatience toward other races or religions, as well as anyone who fell outside of his approval led to diminishing of the circle of those who would tolerate him. Not understanding he contributed to this widespread reaction, he grew impatient and even more negative toward the world outside of his approval.

It did not take long for his emotional, mental, and physical health to deteriorate while he continued to blame all around him for behaviors he could not agree with – although they were perfectly acceptable by society's standards. He blamed people for their tolerance and acceptance of other races and religions, political beliefs that he did not share, and even decisions made by groups unrelated to him. Where his influence could not be felt, he found fault. Progressing to hate increasingly remote groups and their causes was his way of attempting to find those that he could influence and sway their way of thinking so that he would be recognized as a leader. The pain of failure at these attempts to build a following resulted in his reaching a breaking point. What followed was further descent into anger, disagreement, and rage at the world around him.

As he became aware of imminent commitment to a medical facility, he was gifted with the awareness that his actions may have come from triggers he was totally unaware of; this was his introduction to the possibility of past life connections.

Agreeing to investigate led to a Journey to Wellness in his life. Finding in his past lifetimes a predilection for assuming personas that were tyrants and tormenters, he visited some to find what led to their becoming this way. Seeing their lives in such a way that revealed experiences leading up to their later identities, he was able to recognize the cycle of cause and effect and feel an understanding compassion for their journeys. That these personas had been created in the image of others and made to become what they did for the sake of power and control – this was revealing and brought clarity to who he was and who he now is. In becoming aware of this pattern, he was slowly able to recognize a positive alternative to his present life attitudes and behaviors.

In time, he shifted his beliefs and trigger responses and relaxed into a more open and accepting personality. As a result, his gradual re-entry into the world of tolerance and compassion led to a new lifestyle, renewed health and wellness, and gratitude for the second chance he received.

In no way was this Journey to Wellness an easy one for him. Beginning as an individual raging against anything considered less-than or inferior to him self, he walked a long road to his recognition of a healthy alternative to his previously chosen reality. Asking questions of his past lives – "was it chosen?" or "was there little or no choice?" involved in his becoming these past personalities – led to an extended period of time devoted, by him, to finding his truth.

He is to be commended for his commitment to this journey, the result of which is life-altering for him self and all those around him. Personal growth comes in many forms, and for him it is now shown in all ways as he is living his best life. In addition, his present life of tolerance and respect for others has translated to his behaviors and actions being noted by others, and he is now seen as an example to live by.

Physical Self-Abuse

Forgiveness of those involved was achieved. She emerged from this darkness with a renewed and cleansed view of her self, her inner strength, her value, her personal power, and her ability to manage it all for a purposeful life.

What is it that makes a person intentionally hurt their self? Sincere belief that they are unworthy, immune to pain, and possibly immortal: this is the curious combination of attitudes that drives self-abusers to test physical limits. They have a perceived need to cut or break or otherwise disrupt the healthy workings of their human body.

This unhealthy mental state is left to mental health professionals to resolve. They give counsel and attempt to understand and eradicate these destructive behaviors. But do they, in the end, fully understand the source and the root cause of a person's need to test their self? That is what the behavior of self-harm is, a test of one's physical stamina, of physical tolerance for pain and continual disruption of the bodily flow of energy. Of course, self-harm is also a cry for help by a person facing a bleak future. Their belief in being unworthy, diminished in the eyes of others, and deserving of pain and suffering is what drives them to these behaviors. Self-abuse is a secretive and silent cry for help that too often is missed.

These behaviors do disrupt the body's energy flow and, thereby, bring into turmoil the necessary equilibrium created by the physical processes flowing beneath the skin. There is a process and a flow and a highly functioning collection of organs that work tirelessly together to maintain bodily health and wellness. To disrupt this flow brings a call for action to the body's defense system and causes a rush to the site of damage by the body's healing mechanisms. In repeating this call to action often, the body's defenses begin to question the reality of subsequent invasions and may not respond as well as in the past. This may become a spiraling down of bodily response and diminished ability to rally against harm.

Our next story to consider is that of a young girl who came into her present life from a collection of trying past times, to say the least, that saw her victimized by many and unable to grow into her own strength and potential. A particular past life she experienced, and still felt deep within her, brought her near to death many times. She expected death to take her often and was sometimes disappointed that it did not, as it would have been a release for her.

While she was controlled by others, she felt that the one area she had control over was her intention to self-destruct. When acted upon, it could remove her from the external victimization she suffered. Did she not see the parallels between being victimized by others and intending to victimize her self? She did not, and it was in this intention to hurt her self that she found a halfway place, where she could feel hurt that fell under her own control. She could cut her self repeatedly where it would not show, and surviving this each time, she felt, made her stronger. Was this intended to arm her against the violence she was experiencing at the hands of others? She believed so and continued on this path.

How did this past experience relate to her present life? There was no need to escape people attempting to victimize her in the present life, but she deeply felt a darkness within her that was unexplained. As she tried to understand this darkness, and feeling of dread, she was led to a type of awareness, an "almost-memory" as she described it, of habitually hurting her self at another time in history, with desperate attempts to escape or overcome violence. This almost-memory became a recurring dream and waking awareness that she could not shake.

Was this a Soul Memory being experienced in the visceral feelings she described? Was it Soul Memory coming to the surface of her consciousness to bring awareness of a link from her past that needed attention, needed healing?

As she came closer to the "almost memory," hazy and not fully seen, she was drawn to experience what it was, thinking that if she repeated what she saw it would go away. Repeating her self-harm was not the answer, but it became a frequent occurrence that took her deeper into self-destructiveness without any awareness of why the original behavior existed.

Taking her through the Soul Healing process opened her to the truth of her history and its link to her present behaviors. As she came to understand what she had attempted to "fix" in her past lifetimes, without success, and as she came to understand the source of her physical and emotional trauma, it was clear to her that she was an innocent participant in that hazy film of her past. Feeling this and knowing this brought a lifting of the dark veil that had covered her vision for too long. She gained a new ability to recognize that she was not responsible for her destructive behaviors, because she had been led to them through actions of others. This epiphany allowed her to begin healing.

That realization grew into her understanding of who she was in that past lifetime, why the experiences at the hands of her abusers were not her fault, and, further, how to recognize her self as victim and not take blame. Forgiveness of those involved was achieved, and she emerged from this darkness with a renewed and cleansed view of her self, her inner strength, her value, her personal power, and her ability to manage it all for a purposeful life. The depth and range of this woman's intention to hurt her self in order to "fix" what was wrong with her was extensive—and her journey was a lengthy one.

When awareness comes through the Soul Healing process that no blame should be accepted, as it did for her, it is just a matter of time until resolution is found. Recognizing one's innocence in past times is the catalyst to releasing personal blame in the present and peeling back the layers of long-held guilt to reveal that innocence. This is the way.

She now understands her Higher Self is with her, and she recognizes this presence and guidance is constant, if she will allow it. This has become her greatest blessing in life, and she is renewed and committed to sharing her wellness lessons and teachings with others in need of healing.

The journey can be short or long, but the process is the same. Open to revelations of what was, and what is, then see the picture of what can and will be. This is the Soul Healing magic.

Gifted or Mentally Ill?

Many consider hearing voices in one's head a symptom of mental illness. We suggest it can also be one's Higher Self sharing guidance.

Encountering people who are gifted, who have the ability to go within for answers and are enabled by their trust in self to be guided by their Higher Selves, this is not uncommon. If they also are enabled to communicate with Spirit, some may find this problematic. Today, such communication is called by different clinical names that denote mental illness.

It has been our experience to find some spiritually communicative people in our society incarcerated, institutionalized, and labeled as mentally unstable or worse. There is a sadness around this, for in communicating with Spirit there is clarity and guidance that does not necessarily portend illness or instability. Indeed, there are those whose inner voices are destructive and lead to behaviors that are negative and damaging. However, there is a balance of people who are gifted with positive and loving communication with Spirit Guides and Higher Selves.

A deeper understanding of intuition can show that inner guidance, the Soul Memory's form of giving guidance, may show itself as a thought or voice coupled with an intuitive feeling. Combined or separate, they are the inner wisdom guidance each person is capable of receiving but may choose to ignore.

We support the deeper investigation each person may take, if they recognize the communication we describe and do not know its origin. Here is where the application of inner strength and personal power should enter your journey. It is important to believe in your self and make your judgement of how your own Spirit communication feels to you. Being aware that it brings guidance in positivity and a feeling of comfort to you, this is validating. It is in recognizing this and trusting the source that you will open to the benefits, including waking to your personal power and Inner Knowingness that you are not alone on your journey. Your Higher Self travels with you, guiding and protecting, always.

For those with little trust in their selves or understanding that they may be guided from within, hearing strong voices and intuitively feeling direction in thoughts and ideas comes as a surprise. All people have inner wisdom and may receive guidance if they will open to it and open to receive without fear or distrust.

It was a sadness to receive communication from a young man who did not believe there was anything wrong with him, but somehow found him self incarcerated in a mental hospital with the label of schizophrenia attached to him.

As he related his story to me by telephone, it became clear that he had fallen on hard times in his life, was quite alone on his journey, and had allowed him self to become despondent. That is when the voices began, he said. They were supportive and positive and intended to guide him to know he was not alone, that he had Spirit guidance, and that he would see his wellness restored in time. This he believed and began to rely on the voices for emotional support. Soon, he found him self referring to this guidance in conversation with others. Was his truth misunderstood by those around him? Indeed, it was. Did he succumb to the misdirected help offered to him by traditional medical sources? He did. He then found him self on a journey through clinical interventions that did not respect his deep trust in Spirit guidance. This added further confusion to his situation, as he was caught between what brought him comfort and those insisting that most powerful source of healing was not to be trusted.

Our conversations supported what he believed, but his confinement did not allow him freedom to follow his chosen path.

While he had interest in learning of his past lifetimes and how his current life was impacted by them, we were given no opportunity to investigate or begin the journey. This brief story of our meeting is intended only to show the fragility of human life and wellness. Current belief in psychiatry and psychological intervention is based on the good work being done around the world. There is a missing link, however, to the true nature of humanity. While this young man believed in his trust in Spirit guidance, he was unable to sufficiently articulate his belief or experiences to the medical professionals involved in his care.

In the end, this young man disappeared into the system, never having been encouraged to explore the possibility that his inner guidance could be working for his own good, that he may not be mentally unstable, rather that he was the beneficiary of love and support from his Soul Wisdom and guidance. Instead, he was medicated, labeled schizophrenic, and kept in confinement; we had no further communication with him.

> *This is the time and place in the journey to*
> *believe in good health and wellness being*
> *the rightful condition of each person.*
> *~Pax*

Healing Residual Past Life Guilt: Another Visit Needed?

Can the guilt and shame we experience be healed? Or is it a matter of more fully understanding and releasing its origins?

This is indeed the question. When a past life is recognized and understood, when what transpired there is viewed and accepted, is there a move toward releasing the feelings that came with knowing guilt?

There are many ways to move forward after finding what triggers today's behaviors and how their origins have shaped you. For each good deed done in those past times, there are some not-so good deeds in our past also. Is it the case that guilt is harbored in the heart and soul to color the wellness of present day living? Once this is felt and acknowledged, it is time to review what has been for the purpose of releasing the feelings of guilt carried within now. They bring heaviness and inability to function fully in the present.

Taking another look, making another visit to the past lifetime that affects the present so deeply, this is the first step forward. Looking honestly and openly at how you have perceived your role in past life situations, accepting the need to become freed from what needs to be released today, this will show you that traces of emotion linger.

We suggest a review of the initial journey to your pivotal past life. Follow the guidelines as set out in your roadmap for the initial visit and know that this time you will see the missing pieces and be able to let go of remaining traces that bind you to that life's experiences. Remaining remnants of your actions, troubling as they were, require communicating to your Higher Self the need to recognize and release that which remains today and manifests in the form of guilt.

Trusting in Self now to show you the way brings faith in your Journey to Wellness. Sometimes, a sweeping broom can miss; not all is cleared out in a single pass. This truth reflects in journeys to your past lifetimes, in isolating what was troublesome and letting go, releasing what no longer serves you. Having a second look and opportunity to sweep away what was missed, this is always available to you. There is never an ending on the Journey to Wellness, as all of your history is there to be accessed, understood, and allowed to become a piece of the past that is respected but not repeated. You have the power to determine what is for keeping and what is for leaving back in time, with love, as you heal from the link to guilt.

What is guilt, really? We say it can be regret. Through understanding the people you were in the past – your motivations, your circumstances, and your influences from those lifetimes – you can recognize the meaning of a situation and come to understand you did the best you could at the time. Allowing understanding to become your reality, then releasing attached emotions such as regret, this allows a clear vision looking forward while knowing that was then, and this is now. You are forgiving and accepting what was, for what it was, and honoring your self now by moving on in your present life in purity of spirit and intention. Healing is the end result as well as acknowledging that you have accepted this transition, which allows for inner peace to find you and light your way into the future.

When it is learned that what was thought needed for us no longer affects what is, the world looks brighter, because it is brighter. A load is lifted from the heart. As the sun rises daily, gratitude can be expressed and a new way of living in joy is found. This is a powerful intention, this striving to live in joy and gratitude. It results in peace and love becoming the dominant emotions to live by and share with others. Through this spreading of love, peace, and joy, the world as a whole becomes the ultimate recipient of your healing intentions.

Like the proverbial pebble thrown into a pond, with resulting ripples spreading to touch all sides, your heart-shared loving energy spreads in this way. It touches the far corners of the energy field that is your world.

Love and peace extend on those ripples you create and share. They are a gift to all.

The Personal Pace of Healing

We choose now to speak of the time it takes for some to find their way to wellness. The first step begins with recognition of the need for change, for healing, and for a life with less anxiety and challenge. Is this a place one arrives at without inner searching and contemplation? We say no. Often, healing takes time for the requisite soul searching to have been completed. Do you ask where this term originated, "soul searching"? Ironic, is it not, that the phrase is considered metaphysical and other-worldly, yet it is commonplace in society? It seems to be one of the expressions widely used but without much appreciation given to the true meaning.

Confidence comes in many ways and always in a person's own time. There is no one-size-fits-all method. Entering into the realization that all can be healed, and self-healed at that, brings surprise and awe for the processes undertaken. It matters not how long it takes to understand, to accept, to begin, or to continue the Journey to Wellness. What brings happiness and fulfillment to one is not measured by the progress of another. This we know and emphasize for all to hear. Peace lives in the heart of each person and is achieved at their own pace.

Finding within one's self the recognition that all is not well or as it could be and should be is the catalyst for deeper introspection and learning. It is during this phase of personal development and growth that the option of directing one's own inner healing becomes known. It is with this awareness that the magic begins.

Yes, we say magic. How else do we describe the illumination of a previously unknown pathway, complete with full explanation of each stage of the process, and guidance all the way through to successful completion? We say it is magic.

> *The inner Self, the Angels flying with you honor*
> *your intentions. and open to the magic. It is known*
> *that Angels dabble in magic; trust where they lead.*
> *~Pax*

Are You Among the Wisdom Keepers?

We wish to provoke interest and heighten awareness of the next stages of your planetary development and where your people will take their lives going forward.

Those who are evolving, learning, opening to receiving wisdom and guidance – these are the new leaders. They feel their development progressing.

Then, there are those who came into your world leading: those who even as children were advanced and capable and carried wisdom and knowledge beyond their years.

Here we describe the gift of a wellness movement, one that works toward mass healing of emotional as well as physical limitations that were not caused by the present lifetime, but rather have been carried in from past life experiences. Recognizing this and accepting that these Soul Memories can be moved away into the ethers, this is also a gift of healing.

Viewing your Earth plane as a school, an Earth school, allows those in need of healing to learn how they arrived there and for what purpose. Some have come to teach, some to learn, some to challenge, some to crusade, and some to fear it all. Life goes on around all these scattered segments of the population, although it spins faster in some circles than others.

How do these different people fit within the Soul Healing teachings?

Some who are reading these words will be nodding in agreement, recognizing their selves in the words and feeling familiarity in what the book has to say. They are the teachers. Those who feel skeptical and withhold their trust in these words, they will challenge. Others who read and agree and trust and take the journey, they will learn and may become teachers who go on to crusade for the healing word to become widely known and followed. Each type of person has value. Each contributes to understanding and spreading Soul Healing practices and knowledge to Earth's people. This is a gift to universal wellness.

Considering the present self as deserving
of healing and of love and support
brings a renewed and heightened sense of self.

Reclaiming Personal Power

Throughout the process of guiding clients through Past Life Regressions, there has been a common reaction, a recurrent theme attached to the outcome that combines surprise with awakening and recognition with gratitude. Awareness of the big picture – the past and present melded with glimpses of the future – this is the gift that comes with clarity.

Clarity is also to be found through the self-guided method of following the Soul Healing process for your self. Opening to recognition and understanding of the origin of present day challenges enables a shift in attitude and release of self-condemnation and blame. Considering the present self as deserving of healing and of love and support brings a renewed and heightened sense of self.

This is the time and place in the journey to believe in good health and wellness being the rightful condition of each person. Finding wellness now is a joy. In this joy comes the desire to pass along more healing to others. We go through our lives with much love to give and too often do not follow through and give, especially to self.

As you progress through the process toward your Soul Healing, we intend that you also find your personal power. If it has been diminished over time or even given away, worse yet taken from you, now is the time to reclaim this aspect of your wellness. Yes, it is part of what is rightfully yours. Without the confidence to claim and believe in your right to hold this power, there will inevitably be a lack of emotional wellness.

You are not intended to go through life lacking trust in your self, your decision making, and your beliefs. This feeling of lack needs healing now. Recognizing your personal strength and integrity means believing in your self, and your Higher Self, and trusting in living your greater good as a constant contributor to wellness on this planet.

For many people, the idea of personal power is foreign, misunderstood, and thought of as merely self-serving and self-centered: anything but the human right it truly is. If this view of personal power describes you, read on. Reinforcement of your rightful Journey to Wellness and taking back your personal power, or perhaps learning it for the first time, is in order. It is a critical building block to your life's rightful happiness and success. We wish to reinforce this now and show the way for those who have taken time and energy to follow the Soul Healing process.

Affirmations for wellness are widely used, situationally by some and daily by others. They are to be considered building blocks for continued wellness, both emotionally and physically, and are important tools throughout this process of Soul Healing. The following affirmations speak of reclamation of personal power as a significant aspect of wellness.

- I visualize and feel my present self healed of past wounds.
- I am in control of my life and my body.
- I visualize and feel my self in prime physical and emotional health.

*Breaking the chains of past life influence,
this is the key to healing.*

We suggest it can be possible to heal habitual poor food choices and eating disorders by healing a past life's trauma experiences. Poor eating habits and mind-body connections to food may not be your fault.

09

Soul Healing for Weight Management

Releasing The Chain

When we speak of Soul Healing for weight management, we encounter a steady stream of people who overeat, undereat, and generally abuse their food-body relationship.

So many individuals we have known do not understand why they are dependent on food as an emotional comfort, why they are fearful of eating food, or why they are unable to view their body shape and size realistically and with acceptance. It is a confusing and desperate situation for many.

We have found, in regressing people through their past lifetimes, that there is direct connection between now and then: between current food tendencies and past life trauma experiences or conditioning. There is often a direct link to scarcity of food in another lifetime; to a need to steal food to feed one's self and one's children; to a damaging food-as-reward situation; to a fear of eating due to body shape and size expectations; or to any number of life experiences that leave a person with an unrealistic and unhealthy relationship with food today. Residual harms from the past are life-altering and controlling without an understanding of why or where they originated.

Consider that eating disorders and poor food habits may be linked to a past lifetime, and that conditioning or wounds experienced then are not the fault of who you are today.

A Transformational Path to Wellness – What to Expect

- We visit pertinent past lifetimes to learn who you were and the source of your current food challenges.
- Through healing of those old wounds, and forgiveness and release from that past, you become free to make wise choices.
- Recognizing and focusing on personal strengths brought forward from your past lives brings empowerment.
- New and liberating responses to old food triggers are created, resulting in greater self-worth and control over your body-mind connection.
- Guiding you to access the strength of your Higher Self-taps into Soul Power, healing, and personal transformation.

Poor eating habits and mind-body connection to food may not be your fault.

A commonly experienced challenge in this world today has to do with food and the unintentional abuse of it. Too much, too little, dangerously little, or dangerously much: each extreme has its own set of perils for the human body and mind.

Where do these triggers originate for people? What causes the need to constantly consume food? Further, what causes a person to fear eating, or to view their body in such a way that it can never be good enough? Each of these behaviors – and that is what they are, behaviors – can be traced to past life conditioning.

As we have worked individually with people to discover their personal reasons for food abuse today, we have found origins in lifetimes of poverty, where stealing and eating food where it could be found was necessary for survival. We have also visited lives lived in great riches of material abundance but in servitude to the demands of others, regarding physical body shape and size. Others found their selves imprisoned where food was rarely offered, or living life as a homeless mother, for example, who needed to steal food for her children. Past lives such as these have all left scars on the psyche of those who lived through them, left the marks of trauma on their Souls, which today result in reactive behavior detrimental to good health and wellness.

There were experiences, living in past lifetimes, when the need to be extremely thin was such that punishment and constant abuse were inflicted on those who developed extra body weight. Today's fears of eating are triggered by memories of past abuse, so that bulimia and anorexia can result. For those who suffer those tragic conditions, without personal fault, eating enough to sustain a healthy body is not considered as important as remaining unsustainably thin.

Through visiting past lifetimes, we can fully understand who we were and the experiences responsible for today's challenges. This insight enables us to identify and release current triggers to over-eating, or fear of eating, and move forward into Soul Healing.

Understanding that we are not the creator of today's weight challenges, that they are rooted in a past lifetime, which we now have the power to change is liberating and empowering.

Have we been conditioned to think that compulsive eating, poor food choices, obesity, fear of food, anorexia, or bulimia are our own fault? Have we been further conditioned to think that we can magically make it all go away with more self-control? We say yes, with sadness.

How often do we try everything within our power to make a change, only to give up eventually and succumb to the feeling of having little or no control over our body, our eating habits, and food in general? We say too often, with sadness.

Only through understanding the root of a problem can we make successful and lasting change. Knowing that the source of our food-related challenges lies in another time and place – and being given the necessary tools to understand our current responses to triggers from that time – this enables us to respond from a position of personal power and with healthy choices.

Moving through our process of Soul Healing provides insight, clarity, and the ability to separate today's life path from previous lives that have, to a degree, controlled us. Most importantly, we can separate out the emotions connected to past wounds, from our current life, to understand, forgive, and release what we once knew and move ahead in freedom to be the person we desire to be.

> *Separation from the past and transformation into the you of today involves healing and growing. Given tools for change, we embark on a transformational Path to Wellness.*

Identification of our pertinent past lifetimes reveals present triggers. Moving into the healing path of forgiveness and release of our past selves from blame returns personal control and power to us. Affirmations for wellness further strengthen that awareness of self-healing and renewed physical and emotional health. Responses to these triggers can be revealed for what they are, then understood and released.

Truly separating our present life from our past allows for transformation. There will be gratitude for the strengths and lessons learned from our past selves as well, which often brings us the necessary structure and stamina to persist on our Journey to Wellness. Changing life habits is never simple. Only when we understand the basis for our response behaviors are we empowered to create a process for change.

Planting personal power seeds is an integral part of the healing process. Believing in one's self is the key to accomplishing anything in life, from the smallest first step to the greatest stride toward the heights of achievement. Often, great achievement lies in taking the first step.

Growing into the person we want to be entails feeling comfortable in our own skin, in our choices, and in our surroundings. Truly feeling appreciation for our strengths – and even weaknesses that we have identified and now released to transform into strength – this is empowering, as is recognizing, and celebrating our progress.

On the journey to Soul Healing for Weight Management, we feel the support that comes from our Higher Self. We feel the progressive healing of our mind and body and transition into feeling purposeful, in control, and grateful for our renewed self. We express gratitude for the abundance in our life and feel blessed that our inner strength and wisdom continue to grow.

As we move through the process, we notice that our eating habits and food choices have changed – almost without thought. Focus in other areas of life grows and improves as attention to food diminishes and loses power over us. No longer being pulled toward or repelled by thoughts of food allows for freedom to choose, wisely and thoughtfully and in our own time. This truly is freedom for those who have been controlled by food wants and not by needs. What we knew was unwise compelled us to give in, when it continued to call to us loudly.

The ability to live well without interference from our past life experiences, this brings a lightness of being and freedom from fear.

We may feel a fear of failure, considering how to overcome something that controls us as much as food does, especially when we have no idea why it is has so much power in our life. Understanding the source of its power enables us to diffuse and release the triggers, regain our freedom, and move ahead into wellness.

Through the healing of our Soul, that which travels with us through lifetimes holding the highs and lows of past experience, we can rise above limitations and challenges and grow into our full potential.
~Pax

Viewing the Past: Stories Told and Healing Found

From Cold Confinement to Chronic Overeating

As we entered into the exploration of this woman's past lifetimes to seek reasons for her dependence on food, it became clear that she lacked discrimination about what or when she ate. She also had no interest in limiting her food intake or altering her food choices, but diminishing good health was reason enough to inspire her to look for help.

As we regressed to her past, I saw her in a concrete cell enclosure, where it was bare and cold, and she was alone. It became clear she had been there for a long time and would be held indefinitely. She was given meagre rations of food. Although fairly regular, they were barely enough to survive. The captors had no interest in her wellness or comfort. There was no warmth, only cold and threat of starvation without hope for change. There was also abuse and cruelty, which led to her becoming desensitized to her surroundings.

In her present life, there was a craving and a clinging to the comfort food provides, to the extent that she reached out constantly for something to put into her mouth. That gave her relief from the inner fear she would starve to death. It was a persistent need, and she was controlled by this need without consciously being aware of it or its origin. Without understanding the source of this food obsession, she was powerless to control it.

Knowing this history now, she can recognize that her life will not end if she has no food in her mouth for a period of time. She is able to disconnect from the magnetic pull, the uncontrollable need to chew, which she did not previously question. Constant eating brought peace and calm. Carrying the excess body weight that resulted from her habits did not feel good, however. Physical ramifications began to take their toll.

The next stage of her healing came through being able to understand her past lifetime situation for what it was. This involved recognizing that the time in which she lived was exceedingly harsh. She was a victim of those times. The way to release her self now, from that grip on her, was to extend forgiveness to her captors and those responsible for her wasting away in a cell.

As we examined the circumstances of her incarceration, she was able to work through the healing process and take her recognition and understanding of that time through to forgiveness and release of attached emotions. Elevating her present self beyond the control of this past life memory was cathartic, liberating, and healing for her in all ways. Today, she has retained the resulting physical and emotional health and wellness.

Now her life revolves around maintaining this wellness, eating a healthy diet, and enjoying the outdoors and exercise as part of her lifestyle. She experiences no triggers tied to her past but remembers the story well enough for it to serve as a reminder that her present life is one to be grateful for. She feels and expresses this gratitude daily: gratitude for what she has learned and the peace in her heart now that continues to transform her daily life. Added to this is the joy she continually experiences in witnessing her return to wellness in all ways, her reclamation of personal power. She now shares lessons with students on their own search for wellness, telling others that with a high level of personal power and a pair of sturdy shoes, one can walk the world in confidence while enjoying the journey.

Long-Term Diet to Long-Term Binge: She Thought She Was in Control

It had become a pattern that this woman's lifestyle included too much food and drink and a feeling that she was immune from gaining weight and losing wellness. This gave way to the reality of needing to eat healthier and exercise more. So began a period of diet that severely restricted food and drink. It was a repeating cycle and pattern that needed to be interrupted. First, however, it needed to be understood, as understanding is the basis for release and healing.

Her journey imparted new awareness of past lifetimes when excesses were the norm. Now the link to those times needed recognition, so the triggers could be released. How do we enter into this process so change can be made? For each of us, looking back can be uncomfortable. But we must know it is also cathartic.

Taking the next step toward wellness begins with the intention to learn what we need to know in order to address our challenge head-on. We have the ability to overcome if we so choose. This process will lead you through to the epiphany, the "aha" moment of understanding, and the beginning of the next chapter of your chosen life.

First, trust that your past holds keys to your present and your future. Perhaps you feel this and have, over time, had strong inclinations that this is the case. It is these clues that let you know you are more than your present – you are very much your past brought forward. Some see little evidence of this. For others there is a direct line, a direct connection to another time. It can seem obscure and hazy, like clouds covering an otherwise clear sky. But those clouds can be parted to reveal what is written behind them. The message is there, as is the history of your Soul. Uncovering its hidden lessons is your gift to your self.

Her journey within and back in time showed her past lifetime personas, much like a film playing out across the screen of her mind. How was she to learn who and what from those times caused her to live in ways detrimental to good health and wellness now? The way for her was to recognize the feeling of what comes while viewing the past moving through different time periods, or at least those that resonated with her. When there is an awareness of familiarity and a response deep within to the scenes shown, this indicates pertinence to today's lifetime.

We then looked more deeply into a particular past lifetime, to find what episodes occurred that were so profound she was still impacted today. By knowing this connection, she could resolve hurt within her own mind and heart, ultimately releasing long-held pain from her memory and bank of emotional triggers.

To be free of these triggers, the need to behave in such a way as was necessary for survival in another life, is liberating. This is what we aim for now. The goal is for you to release your self from the need to react to suffering that may have occurred centuries ago.

Think of that! Freedom and the ability to go forward in complete control over your present selves is the outcome of Soul Healing.

When she approached the process in a structured way, this woman was able to follow it like numbered bricks along a pathway. This worked well for her. She released her past as she progressed, also recognizing that she was taking back her power: the personal power she had given away so long ago. This felt particularly good to her, and at each stage she was further empowered to know her future would be free of what did not serve her well. This was the choice that allowed her to move forward into the next chapters of her life without lingering control from her past selves.

The earlier lifetimes' lack of control, which caused her to abuse food and drink today without fear of negative outcomes, this was finally understood for what it was: over-reaction to being deprived and needing to exert her own authority over this aspect of her life. She abused her physical health through excess, seeing her loss of control as control. Unfortunately, the result was loss of physical wellness. Because she continued to live with one foot in a time when choices were not hers to make, she took her misguided sense of personal control to a harmful excess. It was a confusing time for her. Her journey to visit that pivotal lifetime allowed the story to open and reveal basic cause and effect. Clarity resulted, as did release of this painful chapter in her history.

Historical Food Stealing and Hoarding – Finding Her Link to Over-Eating Now

As we entered into discussion with this next woman, it became clear she had a history she did not understand, one which affected her present behavior. That history came from a past lifetime, one she agreed to explore.

As we regressed back to that time, it was obvious that had been a time of poverty and almost complete lacking for her. The only positive force in her life was her children, however they were a small blessing, as she was ill-equipped to care for them. Having neither financial nor emotional wellness, she was living in poverty and pain, without support from anyone and without income with which to buy food. So began the practice of stealing, which she was forced to do in order to feed her children and her self.

She saw her self in her daily travels in that lifetime throughout the city where she lived, wearing rags and walking the cobblestone streets trying to not be seen. She would take advantage of situations where she could reach out to street-vendor stalls and take food. Always vigilantly searching for more and maintaining heightened awareness of where there may be something within reach – this took a toll. The stealing extended beyond food, eventually, as there were other unmet needs for her self and her children. It was a cruel life.

Her inability to provide the basics for her children, combined with fear of starvation, left her with negative tendencies in this present lifetime: deep feelings of inadequacy and guilt, a need to hoard food, and a habit of eating more than was needed to sustain her body. None of these behaviors were understood by her until the visit to that lifetime, where she could view her self in the situation where she was powerless and without resources but with children to nourish and protect.

When it was revealed how she came to be in that place of poverty and aloneness, without support or another adult to lean on, she was able to know her full life story. Recognizing the journey she took and how she arrived there was instrumental in her accepting the facts of that time. Knowing that she could be released from the hold of that lifetime through understanding and forgiveness of those involved in her pain and suffering was liberating. So, she worked on developing that understanding, that forgiveness, and was successful in separating her self permanently from the connection to that painful life. She removed that link in her personal life chain and healed her Soul connection from past to present.

Royalty and Body Image – The Binge-Purge Cycle

She had been a royal in a past lifetime. This we learned early in our exploration of her earlier lives. She lived in a time when, although she was a royal, as a woman she was powerless over her future. Even her daily life fell under the control of others. She was there to please, to produce children, and to provide amusement. She was expected to be the envy of all other royals and those who served them. Her beauty was only external and for others to look upon and marvel at, to appreciate and envy and to place on a pedestal. Her appearance and comportment had to exemplify the epitome of wealth and refinement, as they were judged at that time.

What we learned together is that food was withheld in order to maintain the reed-thin appearance so valued by her peers. When she did find food, she was afraid to touch it, afraid of swelling beyond the thin persona required for her lofty station in life. If she did eat, she felt the need to purge it from her body out of fear of weight-gain. This set her up for a lifetime of fearing food and its effects on her body, in favor of the approval and security that compliance with strict rules brought her. She would have been removed from her comfortable life had she deviated from her mandated appearance. That past life was comfortable in one way, yet most uncomfortable in others, as personal unhappiness overtook her wellbeing.

In her present life, she could not understand her fear of eating that contradicted the need for physical wellness and nourishment. She faced a complex set of circumstances that no amount of counselling had enabled her to understand the source of. This is where we began our search to find the origin of her unhealthy relationship with food.

Because she was able to view the film of her past lives, she recognized the lifetime and experiences responsible for her present day food triggers. This was an epiphany for her. The realization came that nothing in her present life could hurt her, in terms of food consumption, and she could release the connection between food and fear. It took a period of adjustment for her to relax into the knowledge that food did not necessarily equate to increased body size or waistline expansion. She gained a relief and a release of that control over her mind-body connection. She felt reborn and, in a profound sense, she was. From then on, her life was lived looking forward, not back. The experience of discovering the source of her former unhealthy relationship with food clarified much for her, and she chose to leave it behind as a constructive memory and focus on a healthy present and future.

She also chose to devote much of her time to speaking of her experiences to others with similar challenges to those she had overcome. She was a valued contributor to solutions for many who had run out of options.

Anorexia, Bulimia, and Food-Body Relationships through Time

The tendency toward these unhealthy behaviors are driven, in part, by today's unrealistic beauty standards and views of body image that encourage people to remain thin beyond what is healthy or able to support life. Past life experiences, where expectations and punishments followed if this unrealistically thin body shape was not attained, these color the present thought and action of many who see their selves as never thin enough and never good enough, as a result.

This is a sadness. Impossible expectations result in suffering beyond the imaginable by those trying to be what a deep, subconscious, and unknown belief demands of them. This is a pull to a place of compromised health and even possible death. Recognizing this for what it is and what it was, knowing it has no basis in reason in this lifetime allows it to be understood and released from any further influence on a present life.

Those who have lived during times when either fashion or fetish demanded extremely thin appearance are left today with memory remnants of punishment they received if their appearance displeased those in control of their life. Those in control made decisions for them and created a life not touched by appreciation or love, particularly when displeasure was shown in order to keep them submissive to the will of others. Trying to find approval and appreciation in a life of harshness and punishment for perceived infractions, including not looking the way one was expected to, this left scars still seen today.

That trauma runs deep in present life, to the extent there is not an understanding of why there is fear attached to food. The need to recognize a pivotal past life, the harshness of it and the treatment received, this enables an individual to come to an understanding of why they suffered, who those people were who brought hurt to them, and what caused their cruelty. The end result is an ability to understand and forgive those involved and release them from continued attachment to today's life. It is a mixed blessing, knowing one's painful history and then using that knowledge to release all traces of what once was. Moving ahead free of these links in the chain of memory is liberating, but the process requires dedicated work. It is also healing for those who persevere.

Recognizing and releasing our connections to the past, looking forward in appreciation of self, in all ways, this brings empowerment and self-love in place of pain.

His Lifetime Food Dependency: Soul Healing Led Him to Self-Mastery

Eating to feel the high, reveling in the high, needing it and constantly thinking about good feelings that come from food – this is the pattern of his food dependency.

More than over-eating, more than the love of food, and more than wanting the feeling of fullness in the stomach: his is a cellular and visceral craving for the feeling of food being chewed, being tasted, being swallowed, and above all being savored. The afterglow from these sensations seeds the next craving and begins the cycle again, a constant need for food's fulfillment. It is as powerful as the craving for drugs or alcohol, although with food being more readily available this craving is more easily satisfied. Perhaps it is this easy availability that contributes to the rapid acceleration of food dependency.

Seeking to illuminate the origins of this dependency in his life, we spoke with this man who had stories to tell about his current life being unhappy from childhood onward. He had been unappreciated always, he felt: not accepted by his peers as he progressed through school. He had no idea why he was alone, and why nobody seemed to care for him. He withdrew into him self more and more and found a friend in food. It was the constant presence of this friend that contributed to his increase in body weight to over 300 pounds. Eventually, walking more than a few steps at a time became impossible. His physical health was compromised almost beyond repair.

Here is the beginning of his descent into what he did not anticipate, which was further isolation from those he knew and any possible way of bringing him self closer to a life lived happily together with family and friends.

Looking into his past and examining the film of lifetimes previously lived showed a succession of what appeared to be lonely and unhappy experiences. Across personas and centuries, he had always felt that he lived on the periphery, outside of what others considered normal. It appeared so. Looking closer to find patterns in past lifetimes that may relate to his current self, he saw clearly that he had created his lifestyles and limitations even then. How deeply did his personal pain extend, and how deeply was that pain felt today? Is there a connection between the two, we asked, and would healing one help to heal the other?

Entering into regression to locate the core and origin of his problems, we found this man to be a mirror image now of who he presented in past lives. Had unhealthy behaviors been a conscious choice then? Was his food dependency a problem for successive selves? If so, what led to it in each lifetime? These question we asked him. Serious self-examination is a powerful tool, and he entered into it wisely. Sharing a clear view into the lifetime holding the key to his initial alienation from the mainstream, we worked through the experiences of that former time and the people who first caused his emotional wounds. Ultimately, he followed the path to understanding, forgiveness, and release.

His Soul Healing process was in no way a "quick fix." It had taken him many lifetimes to descend deep into the abyss of loneliness, so he allowed him self much time to work on his release from the hold those past times had on him now. He was wise enough to recognize what he had created; it was now clear to him. He would do all in his power to move past the past and into wellness – which he did.

Returning freedom to him self was his greatest gift. Allowing exploration of life without isolation, life where return to wellness became his priority, and finding he was not alone in this journey – these newfound joys propped him up to the extent that he became able to function without the crutch of needing food for fulfillment. In fact, he went on to reach out to others and share the truth: there is a way out of such bondage as he had created for him self.

Believing in his worth, his value, and his deservedness of a life lived through sharing joy with others as friends, he worked to return to him self the personal power long ago relinquished. Now he could see; the lack of his intention to function in wellness was the missing piece to his life puzzle. Over time, he completed the puzzle's picture and trusted in him self to be worthy of all that is good in life. This worth he reclaimed, then went on to teach his story of self-mastery. He is now an inspiration to many.

The Thread of Life Contained in Soul Memory

The stories we have just relayed show that it is the thread of life contained in Soul Memory that keeps us connected to our past. If we can recognize that the pushes and pulls of current life have a basis in the reality of who we have been, and that we are not now subject to the pain of that time, then we can witness the film of past lives as it plays out but not be hurt by it or experience any discomfort. Protected from past hurt, we can understand and learn from what our Spirit Guides reveal. The Soul Healing process allows the viewer to release the hold of past times on the present. This is the tool that allows the conscious mind to understand there is no shortage of food now, so moderation can be achieved.

It is the breaking of a chain, one link at a time, that allows transformation to wellness.
~Pax

Will You Choose a High Road or Low Road?

Going forward on the Soul Healing Journey to Wellness, there is love and support from your Higher Self, always. Know this is a strong support pillar of your Soul Healing journey, but its power is not limited to this process alone. Rather, you are also guided and protected along your daily journey to a happy and healthy life.

Can it be said that for each person who falls between the cracks of wellness there is lacking in their belief in deserving of the best for their selves? We say the high number of those experiencing dis-ease, in some way, feel they deserve less than total wellness. This is unfortunate, and a sadness in your world today. How is it that so many people experience this lack?

We do not dwell on the deeper reasons now but move on to the importance of finding the trust in self, and Higher Self once again, to undertake the journey up and over the wall that has confined so many to this negative attitude and outcome. You are what you think you are. Therefore, set a course to the high road or the low road and, either way, you will achieve that on which you focus.

We say it is as direct a route, whether to the high road and wellness or to the low road and all that it brings. So, why would you choose the low road? Think on this question. Why would you knowingly choose a direction that takes you down and away from wellness, happiness, fulfillment, and a future to be chosen for its wealth of promise? Or, if you see your self traveling that path, not being consciously aware of how you arrived there, know that you can change course and set as your target the high road to happiness and wellness. Help is yours to claim on this journey.

Habitual choices that are influenced by past life experiences would be one reason for gravitating to the low road. How is it that the cord is so strong that influences on today, from the past, can barely be resisted or managed? There is need to understand the origin of the trigger and need to release the associated reactions. This is your personal power returned and rebuilt and not to be denied.

It is also to be known that your direct link to communicating with your Higher Self remains open and yours to claim. Do you feel the significance of this in your life now? Can you imagine life without this ability to access your inner wisdom? This is one of the greatest gifts to be given. We ask you to consider this truth, guard it, and respect it. Inner guidance is there for you, always, and will lead you in the best direction for your self, always. Your role is to grow your trust in this process.

Who Speaks Loudest, Your Heart or Your Head?

How often have you had a feeling about something but allowed your thinking to be the decision maker instead? These are the two directions that compete for your attention in the decision-making process. One is the intellectual aspect of each choice: what your thinking tells you. The other is the heart's knowing, the intuition, the voice inside you offering to guide. Do you typically follow your thinking or your feeling?

Consider some of your important decisions and what motivated them. Then consider the outcomes of those decisions. Were they positive or negative? You may be surprised to find that your heart has been your best guide. Knowing this and trusting this truth brings renewed empowerment.

To recognize the gift of having your life guidance and answers within you, and your innate ability to access them at will – all this brings a sense of wellness and enhanced personal power. You are free to live and love and find your way through the maze of life, knowing your feet are firmly on the road to your best outcome at all times. What a gift this is!

You are what you think you are. Therefore, set a course to the high road or the low road. Either way, you will achieve that on which you focus.

A healing journey of any kind can be an adventure. Some like to go alone while others prefer travel with a guide. The Soul Healing process is aided by your inner guidance.

Know that you journey with your Higher Self as guide, your greater wisdom and protector, entering onto this healing path wrapped in love and trust.

Observing your past lives and finding those impacting your life today begins the healing of your present – this is our gift to you now.

~Pax

10

Soul Healing: Accessing Your Inner Guidance

This Soul Healing process is based on the premise that past lifetime experiences can be responsible for today's challenges. Through understanding and releasing these past wounds, we can move forward in optimal emotional and physical health and wellness.

We share with you now the pathway and instruction for accessing your inner guidance, your inner compass that comes with love and joy for your present and your future. We share this gift and encourage all to take it to heart, to access it as needed.

Poor eating habits and mind-body connection to food may not be your choice.

When communicating one-on-one with clients, we have used this Four-Stage Process with great success. It is just that, a process, and can be considered a method of behavior modification rather than dieting.

The self-guided methods defined earlier in this book detail steps to connecting with your Higher Self and viewing past lifetimes. You choose the method to use when beginning your journey to find recognition and understanding of who you were in a pertinent past lifetime, the trauma you experienced, and how it relates to the challenges of today's life. This is the basis for a Soul Healing journey.

First, consider what needs healing and why. Then the pathway toward resolution opens. By this, we mean not just your present challenges regarding food but any current life challenges.

Your journey may be self-guided, but you are never alone. You will be able to feel that you are not alone. In this place of connection with your Higher Self is love and acceptance, protection and the wisdom of the ages surrounding you in your quest for wellness. This is the strength of the journey and the assurance that you can undertake it in trust. A renewed you is the goal, and the support of your Higher Self is the assurance of your fulfillment.

You can follow a step-by-step process to address your challenges. It begins with visiting the pertinent past lifetimes where food became a focus. Then comes identifying trigger responses and working through the healing path by using affirmations for wellness and planting personal power seeds. Developing an attitude of gratitude and regularly speaking your appreciation for having released the chain of past life influence – this creates a positive mindset and continues healing.

This complete process has been shared with you here, so an in-depth Journey to Wellness, complete with reviews and revisits, can be undertaken as you so choose.

Each session should be undertaken days or weeks apart, allowing as much time as required for reflection, deep understanding, and acceptance. Ensuring your comfort and understanding that you control this journey is most important. There is no need to rush through the stages. The right time to progress to the next step is when you feel you have released what was presented but still feel a need to find out more. Perhaps a different lifetime impacts the you of today. When you feel ready to address more of your past and strengthen your confidence, that is the right time to make further progress.

For an individual beginning this exploration, following a self-guided process is your portal to past-life viewing. It is effective and recommended.

Combining it with the Four-Stage Process brings enhanced awareness for your deeper journey and creates a measured and steady pace of growth into healing.

To each person who has the intention to seek their inner guidance, we say there is a gift awaiting your entry into the process. Ask for quiet of mind and physical space. Allow inner feelings to become part of your awareness. Further, allow your self to listen for thoughts and feel your heart's intuitive messages. Combined, thoughts and feelings bring a sense of purpose and direction. It is the combination that produces vision now: heart and mind, the intellect and your heart-knowing guidance. The choice of how to meld the two is yours. Listen for messages in thoughts and feel guidance. It will be clear that one or the other is strongest within you and also that they can combine powerfully to form your way forward. The combination of hearing and feeling guidance is yours to receive.

It is your heart that will tell you how it feels about the choice you are about to make. If you feel comforted by the direction you consider or uncomfortable with it, a visceral reaction is immediately recognizable as your guide forward in all aspects of life.

This is a tool that will always guide toward the healing direction you need if you will trust in it. In so doing, you trust in your Higher Self, this guide to Soul Wisdom that travels with you through lifetimes and leads toward your wellness, always.

The process for a self-guided visit to your past lifetimes is repeated here, for ease of following through each part of this four-stage process.

Entering the Portal: Your Journey to Past Lifetimes Begins

Look upon this opportunity to heal now as a gift you give to your self. Wrap this gift in the peace and quiet of a chosen place and time where you will not be disturbed, and your surroundings are quiet and comfortable.

- Sit quietly and comfortably with feet on floor and eyes closed.
- Focus on breathing, only your breathing, in and out regularly, breathing in peace and calm, breathing out any cares of the day. Feel the peace fill you and allow it to envelop you completely until you feel calm, relaxed, and ready to receive.
- Feel the Earth's energy vibrations rising up through your feet into your body and circulating throughout. Visualize the cosmic golden energy cord extending from the heavens down through the top of your head and your Crown Chakra. Feel that energy flowing into and filling your body with love and light. Visualize and feel healing energy flowing through you from both sources: up from Mother Earth through your feet and legs, and down from the heavens through your Crown Chakra. They meet and fill your body with peaceful energy, swirling and melding like two rivers meeting and flowing together as one.
- Feel the tingle of this healing energy being absorbed and imagine it, visualize it filling you, circulating, and settling into your body like an electrical current activating. Feel the peace, feel the calm, feel the love.
- Visualize and feel the energy field encircling you now, creating a glittering and glowing field of love and protection all around the outside of your physical body. Know you are encircled by love and protection for your journey.
- Connect with this power of Mother Earth and the Universal Consciousness – this allows for wisdom and guidance to flow through you, and for you, to become one with your Soul.
- Begin with breathing into your heart the intention to open your self to resolve a present life challenge by finding the past life source of it. Breathing in and out, focus on the intention to recognize, understand, and heal from it.
- In thoughts or words, ask for your Higher Self to be your guide in identifying the past life you most need to visit. Ask to visit that

specific and pertinent lifetime connected to the challenge of today that you intend to understand and resolve. Ask that your visit be made as an observer, that no discomfort or negativity from that time be felt by you now.

- Open your heart to receive this guidance in thoughts, pictures, or feelings; each person receives in their own way. As you do, focus and stay with what comes to you: this picture in your mind or feeling in your heart. Begin to feel this persona and see them in your mind's eye. Take time to settle in with this vision, or feeling. Take the time needed to feel comfortable with this connection to the you of another time, with what you see, and what you feel from it.
- Visualize and feel your self in this past life and who you then were. This will reveal much about that lifetime. Look also to where and what were your surroundings. Get a feel for the you and the circumstances of that time in the place you see. Does it look familiar?
- Is there a specific situation underway that you are involved in, or that you are present in as an observer only? Perhaps you are alone in the scene? Do you feel the potential for danger in any way? Are there others in your picture that are interacting with you? If so, notice your place in the story and what is coming your way. Is there something or someone you recognize that connects with your present day life?
- Begin to sense your emotions of the time; they translate now as thoughts, and you will feel no discomfort as you view the scene as an observer. See and feel the picture and where you are in it. View this scene as a stage play. It is a view into that lifetime and your place in it. What is the scene showing that relates to today's challenge? Focus on the scene shown in your vision and your part in it.

Meeting Your Past Self – A Presence in Both Worlds

- Speak in thoughts or in words to the person you then were or to your Higher Self as guide, asking to understand what they are experiencing. You may have the sense of being in both places simultaneously, and you are. This enables you clear vision while remaining protected from feeling emotion.
- You may experience a feeling of being immersed in a scene from a past lifetime while being aware of the clock ticking in the present.
- Observe the situation and ask clearly why you are involved and what are you to learn from this experience. What is the message embedded in it? Listen in your thoughts for the response and open to hearing or feeling the story. Perhaps dialog is not to be in this case, and your understanding of what transpired, and why, will come through feelings. This may be how you best receive your history. Either way will enable you to connect the awareness of that experience to your present self.
- Is there trauma happening to you? Is there loss or sadness? Is there something causing fear to be felt? Is there inability on your part to fulfill obligations or protect loved ones? Past trauma experiences that could be triggered by today's events are to be examined and understood, for without true recognition of cause and effect there will be difficulty in finding resolution.
- Can you truly understand the circumstances of this past trauma situation, your place in it, and its connection to your present day life? Is it sufficiently clear that you can relate it to your present day triggers? There is a need for clarity here and enough time given to fully understand the connection.
- This is where communication with the you of that time in history can bring clarity and allow for your next steps toward understanding and accepting what was, and to releasing those involved from

blame. It is with this release that you are able to begin the Soul Healing process. Those involved can then be forgiven for their actions, and it may be that forgiveness also needs to be extended to the person you were at the time, who may have acted badly toward others. When you are clear on this connection, truly understand and feel how that situation affects you today, then you can release the link in your chain to that past experience. You can leave your past self with thoughts of love and forgiveness and visualize the broken link in the chain being released into the ethers.

- You can also ask your Higher Self for guidance in moving forward in your present life in wellness. To recognize and understand the picture you saw, feel the energy of the time and release your connection to it. This is the intention. Speaking your words of forgiveness, releasing all involved completes the process. Truly feeling your words in your heart as intention, this is your commitment to the you of your past, present, and future.
- Be thankful for the connection with your past self and extend gratitude for the clarity received. Your past and present selves have both chosen to release your connection, except where it can be beneficial for you today. You may also end your dialog with thanks to your past self for opening to share your history.
- Extend gratitude to your Higher Self for its guidance and protection during this journey, then formally close the session with love and gratitude. It is a gift and a blessing to make this connection and should be respected as such.
- Following this session to connect with a past lifetime experience, there should be a period of contemplation and quiet time to absorb what has been shown to you. This will have been an extraordinary experience and no doubt come with a jolt of awareness. You will benefit from taking time to consider the larger meaning of this new awareness, how it impacts your current life, and how it heals your past as well. One is connected to the other – the present and

- your past – and both will heal if you allow it. Less understood, but just as true, is the healing this release brings to your future.
- Allow this experience, and what you saw and felt, to permeate your body and Soul now. You have been altered with this knowing: added to and enriched as a result. Time must be allowed to pass while the ensuing emotions settle within you. What has been felt and witnessed is a gift, and what has been learned will enable you to grow and heal within your current life trajectory.
- Give your self the gift and the blessing of speaking affirmations to bring comfort, closure, and confirm your intention of going forward in wellness.
  - I am thankful for the wellness and abundance in my life now.
  - I am blessed that my Higher Self guides me on my Path to Wellness; inner strength and wisdom are with me on this journey.
  - I can visualize and feel my present self healed of past wounds.

The Expanded Four-Stage Process shown in the following pages has been used for the benefit of my in-person client's sessions specific to weight management. It formed the basis for in-depth and repeated visits to ensure all negative areas of past lives entered were illuminated, examined, understood, and released.

This process can be followed substituting any current life challenge for the references to food.

The steps shown are concise and a guide for your use in repeated past life regression sessions on your own. They include reminder questions to ask your self, ensuring you covered all needed areas to achieve your goal and that true understanding and release were achieved. Affirmations and personal power seeds form an important part of closure, so they are an integral part of the process.

Encounters with your past selves are the steppingstones to all the gifts that will be experienced through the Soul Healing process. Each time a past life visit is planned, prepare your heart and mind for the journey.

Always ask for the presence of your Higher Self, and you will be guided and protected. Open to receive the awareness and clarity to come.

Blessed Wellness

It is our way
It will be yours
Set the intention
Visualize and Feel
Believe and Trust
We feel the healing energy within us
We expel the healing energy on our breath for others
Blessed wellness we hold in our hearts and minds
Blessed wellness we send as intention to others
We surround our selves with the white light of loving protection.

From The Divine Wisdom Source, Pax.
A reminder that we each have the power.

The Expanded Four-Stage Process

This Soul Healing process follows the belief that past lifetime experiences are responsible for today's challenges. Through understanding and releasing those old wounds, we can move forward in optimal emotional and physical health. This is a guide to revisiting the hard questions, and affirmations, as needed.

Session 1: A Transformational Path

- **Identify** and visit pertinent past lifetimes and experiences and ask:.
  - Who was I?
  - What was the challenge then that I still carry with me today?
  - Who was responsible for my past life trauma?

- Are any of those people present in my life today?
- Is my present connection to food a repeat of past life behaviors?
- Can I understand and release the past with love and forgiveness?
- May I receive guidance to move forward in wellness now?

- **Recognize** Today's Trigger Responses
  - Unhealthy food choices
  - Fear of food intake leading to weight gain
  - Constant need for food as comfort
  - Feeling a lack of self-worth and control
  - Acceptance of powerless state
  - Loss of self-esteem

- **Healing Path**
  - I am not the creator of this, and I can change it.
  - I understand my past trauma and infuse my past self with love.
  - I recognize and forgive those who harmed me.
  - I know I am free to move forward in wellness.
  - I visualize and feel my present self, healed of past wounds.
- Knowing those past life experiences have no power over me today brings release and freedom from food triggers.

- **Affirmations for Wellness**
  - I am healed of past wounds and memories.
  - I am in control of my life and my body.
  - I visualize and feel my self in prime physical and emotional wellness.
  - Other than to fuel my body, I have no desire for food.

Session 2: Separation and Transformation - Review

- Have you brought forward lessons learned in that lifetime?
- Did you forgive and release those past life personas in love?

- Do you know you have been released to live well today?
- Have you chosen to release your past connections, except where they can be beneficial to you now? Do you feel this release?
- You retain only that which will serve your highest and best good.

- **Healing Path - Revisit Trigger Responses for Change**
  - My food quantity and frequency of eating are improved.
  - Now, I make healthy food choices.
  - I no longer reach out for food as comfort.
  - I enjoy an improved self-image.
  - I have reclaimed my personal power.
  - I use powerful affirmations for strength.
  - I believe and trust in my self to make good life decisions.

- **Affirmations for Wellness**
  - I am not the creator of this, and I can change it.
  - I am in control of my life and body.
  - I visualize and feel my Soul Healing.
  - I make wise choices to honor my self.

- **Personal Power Seeds**
  - I value my self highly and choose to maintain my physical and emotional self in alignment with optimal health.
  - I give thanks for the wellness and abundance in my life now.
  - I feel blessed that my Higher Self guides me on the Path to Wellness and supports me in wisdom and inner strength.
  - I trust my renewed self to manage present challenges.

Session 3: Growing and Healing

- Revisit past lives as needed to ensure complete separation.
  - I feel appreciation for areas of strength and weakness in my self identified through past life visits; these have now enabled

me to release emotional and physical connections to previous poor food behaviors.

- **Self-Healing**
    - Visualize and feel your Soul healed.
    - Feel the healing of your mind and body, cell by cell.
    - Know you are a butterfly emerging now into sunshine, to fly.
    - You are loved ; you are appreciated; you are powerful. Feel this.

- **Maintenance Path**
    - Appreciate your present self and progress on this Path to Wellness.
    - Visualize and feel your self in prime physical and emotional health.
    - Feel your personal power attached to this image and state.
    - Lock in and hold onto this feeling and belief.
    - Know you are supported on this path by your Higher Self.

- **Repeat Affirmations of Worth**
    - I am in control of my life and body.
    - I value my self highly and choose to maintain my physical and emotional self in alignment and optimal health.
    - I feel that my Soul is healed.
    - I honor my Self by living as my best self.
    I am thankful for the wellness and abundance in my life now.

Session 4: Review and Reinforce

At this time, we address areas of challenge that may remain, such as:

- Diminished self-esteem
- Unwillingness to believe in what is deserved
- Inability to change detrimental food habits

- Incomplete forgiveness or release of past life experiences or people
- Succumbing to unresolved habits and food triggers.

If any of these challenges continue to be experienced, they indicate that the Soul Healing process requires repeating, with particular focus on specific incidents in your past. You are not alone in this; ask your Higher Self, your guide, to help identify where you need to go, which lifetime remains connected negatively to your present.

Next, begin the review of where release is needed. Infuse that self and lifetime with love and repeat earlier stages of this process, as needed, to break the chain to that which is so strong it continues to impact you today. Know that your personal power is such that you can take this step successfully.

Revisiting pertinent past lifetimes to further explore what transpired then that is so powerful it continues to impact the present – this is your intention. There needs to be clarity and understanding of who was involved, what was the situation and experience, how you were traumatized, or who you may have traumatized. It is then that the process of recognition, forgiveness, and release can once again be spoken, be felt, and be instilled in your Soul for the healing process to unfold.

Complete honesty with your self about your role in past life trauma is needed. Recognition and acceptance of that role allows for release of blame, for forgiveness of self and all concerned. This is the basis for your love of self, and Self, to be rekindled and grown into self-trust and love that is powerful and unshakable through whatever comes in your present and future.

There is no perfect timeline for working through this process to what could be, and when, because each person is unique. Understanding and progressing along the Path to Wellness is a personal journey of discovery. The butterfly appears when it is ready to fly.

As you travel this path, it is recommended to not rush the journey. It may have taken lifetimes or centuries, even, to reach the point where needing help was recognized. So, give patience to this process.

Regular review of each step brings truth and awareness of your progress. Have you given sufficient time to understand what you have learned? Have you truly worked through the process of forgiveness? Did you release your past and accept your new and improved circumstance? Do you deeply know that you control your present and future without this past life connection?

Take time to proceed through each stage at your own speed of understanding and healing. That is important for reclaiming validation, love, and trust in self. This journey takes place between your present self and your Higher Self as guide, and no expectation or timelines should be attached.

- As personal eating habits change into what is healing and supportive for your wellness, remember to visualize and feel your body's organs rejuvenating. Feel the laughter of cells receiving nourishing food in optimal quantities.

- **Abundance and Gratitude**
    - I am blessed that my Higher Self guides me on my Path to Wellness.
    - Inner strength and wisdom are with me on this journey.
    - I am thankful for the wellness and abundance in my life now.
    - I am in control of my life and body.
    - All is well with my Soul.

Wellness is yours to claim and is your due. Know this. Go forward in love and trust for your present self's willingness to so do.

Understanding that you are not the creator of today's challenges but do have the power to make change is liberating. Truly separating your present life from your past allows for transformation.

—Pax

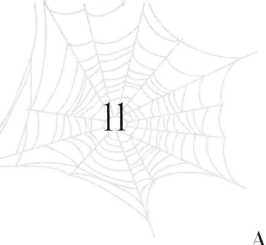

11

After the Epiphany

A Personal Reflection:
Healing the Crack in Her Soul

I invite you to follow the description of experiences shared by a woman who undertook the Soul Healing for Weight Management process with me in person, in repeated sessions, to address her dissatisfaction with excess body weight and poor eating habits.

She reflects on what she found in her pertinent past lifetime, who she was, and how this personality influenced and impacted her still. How was she able to release this past, in care and love for her past persona? This is a pathway she wishes to share for the benefit of others.

Through her inner journey, she learned the identity of a woman she was in a past life: one who became the basis of her knowing the circumstances of how she was traumatized then and how she still carried the marks of that time, emotionally. Her past life persona was named Meg. Through establishing a relationship with Meg, she had conversations and sharing of feelings that led to her healing.

She writes:

"I realize, from personal experience and from observing others, that weight loss is a challenge that all people handle differently and measure it to various extremes. Our sessions with Pax allowed me freedom and knowledge to a degree that I did not anticipate.

Viewing the process agenda in advance, I knew we would be looking into how my Soul Memories may have affected the way I now think about and treat food. I can describe my self as a person who eats randomly and voraciously for no reason. Not hungry? I eat anyway. Too much food on my plate? Too bad, I'm going to eat it all.

With a new awareness that I was an abused, starved, and dominated woman in my far past, and that woman, Meg, was still influencing my survival instinct to hoard and eat anything edible, I not only was amazed but somewhat relieved.

I am not one to lay blame for many things. So, this news helped me to think that my problem was not all mine, but that I shared it with this woman of my past. This was confirmed. What I came away with was both relief and acceptance.

During the next few days, I thought about this past self of mine quite often and explained to her that I was fine, that she too should feel relieved that she was now released from the necessity to 'eat to survive.' I pictured her originally as bedraggled, exhausted, and drawn. By the time the week was out, the image of her that I carried was of a healed lady, with a healthier look, and in a much more pleasant frame of mind and body. I wished her well each time I thought of her, with love and acceptance.

Going forward from there, I was much more aware of the times and circumstances of when and what I was eating. You had asked me to picture the crack in my Soul and to notice it healing. I had a bit of a problem visualizing this but did understand what was meant.

At our next session, I felt that this woman I had been would now be released and a permanent separation would occur. I could now begin to rely on my self and not fear my past and its negative influences. The path was now mine to work on and know that some of the pressures and feelings should be leaving me. I will be able to accept and enjoy the positives gained from knowing my past self.

We talked about affirmations and that I have begun using them to a greater degree. We talked about moderation and that I was obviously not practicing that with eating. The days that followed this session brought heightened awareness of what I was eating and when. I was more at peace with myself.

Entering the next session, I realized that I had not thought of my past self at all since the last session. That came as a surprise to me because I had not noticed it until you asked me about Meg. I find that my mind is now more clear about correct eating and what that means for me.

I believe that the review of each session and of my previous thoughts will be of great assistance. I found benefit in revisiting my sessions regularly and reviewing the changes I experienced in my approach to food. Now I feel in control of food urges and impulses and understand their source.

How something so powerful originates in another century is beyond my understanding. I just know that in recognizing it and releasing it, I am no longer controlled by it. I have moved on.

Choosing to use selections from my personal power seeds brought increased strength of mind and purpose. These seeds of wisdom are helpful in all areas of life, and I use one or more, daily."

Personal Power Seeds

- I have released and forgiven my past self with love.
- I have been released to move forward in wellness.
- I visualize and feel my present self healed of past wounds.
- Those past life experiences are gone and have no power over me today.
- I am in control of my life and my body.
- I visualize and feel my self in prime physical and emotional health.
- Other than to fuel my body, I have no desire for food.

Claiming your personal power and stepping into your truth, your intended identity, this is the joy to be found in your Journey to Wellness

Living the Empowered You

Your journey to wellness has been successful and life resumes with a fresh look. Does this mean there are no more triggers to be encountered or thoughts taking you back to negative reactions? No, it does not. But what it does mean is these triggers can be observed by you but not felt. Your thoughts can be heard and recognized for what they are – but not acted upon. You are now detached from the action itself, an observer only. Allowing the moment to pass without your attention being given to it, this is now your way. It is only a fleeting excerpt from the movie of your past life, which deserves little attention or reaction. You control the film reels. Stop them when you wish.

The triggers are out there but no longer touch you, although it is good to remember that the change is within you and not in the external world. Remembering this allows for awareness that there will be occasional triggers along your path but also the awareness that they, too, are external and cannot control or harm you.

As we consider the ways of avoiding what were previously your challenges, we suggest avoidance is useful but that personal healing is the best path to success. We choose to speak of your inner wisdom and guidance, and how tapping into this brings you direction going forward. When there is need to diffuse a memory situation, your Higher Self knows the way.

Taking a moment to go within and feel the love and guidance there for you – this provides support and confirmation that you are never alone on your journey, never. Trust in this.

As you move forward in renewed health and wellness, remember:

You came into this life with a purpose. You are empowered to recognize it and activate your plan to reach that potential.

Did you come into this world with strengths, gifts, and talents brought forward from past lifetimes? Accessing these can be a surprise and a joy. They bring fulfillment to your present life.

It is not a surprise, then, to learn you have a talent of great proportions. Excellence in art, music, sports, performance, writing, academics, leadership: these strengths are talents and gifts. For many people, there has been a sense that they would like to explore a certain activity when they have time. What draws a person to a specific interest in life? Is it that they feel called to try it, and do they sense they will excel at it? Is it due to a direct link to their past and perhaps a life of excellence in that pursuit? We say that is often so.

Gifted Old Souls Need Healing Too

Those coming into this life as children with the wisdom of an Old Soul, or the talent of a long-experienced professional, are prime examples. Often referred to as "child prodigies," they possess the skills and talents, maturity, wisdom, and presence of one far beyond their years and experience. Is this a random case of unexplainable abilities? We are of the belief that this is not so, that there is a direct connection between these children, who defy explanation, and who they have been in other lifetimes. Along with their advanced knowledge and talents, they bring memories of past lives and times that are not understood by the adults around them. It becomes clear, when investigated, that they bring teachings and experiences from other places and times in history. Sharing their Soul Memories is a positive process that becomes a gift to people of the present time.

Those who experience the beauty of art or music and those who experience the beauty they find in achieving intellectual pursuits–can readily accept that these children are gifted beyond what can be reasonably explained as current life learning. This extends to academics, sports, and all areas where knowledge or achievement surpasses what is considered normal. It is a masterful achievement when those showing their gifts come into this life, and we can explore and learn and take from it what we will. The joy is in finding the true origin of the story.

Coming into this world and this lifetime as an Old Soul has both blessings and challenges. With the gifts of knowingness and intuition comes recognition that life will be somewhat different for the person who possess these capacities-than for others. It is in this difference that separation exists. Although this is positive, there is a need to develop personal power to accept this as a gift and focus on the self and Higher Self. Yes, each of you has a Higher Self and inner wisdom guiding you through the maze that is your current life. The inner voice you often hear, or sense, that guides to do or not do – this is your inner and greater wisdom, your Higher Self watching over you. There is no doubt you have heard and responded and later wondered about it. That you took heed is the lesson, as is recognition of the positive outcome of this guidance for you at that time.

Life is a balancing act, or it should be. To find the middle way, you may have need to release certain connections to your past that bring dis-ease. This is not to be feared. Your ability to access your past is within your control. While exploring your past lives for this purpose and communicating with your past selves, you may also ask to view your past achievements and strengths, talents, and those gifts that made those times special and memorable in good ways. All that you have been through and all your past successes add to the full sense of who you are today. That knowledge, in itself, is a gift.

Stepping Into Your Truth

Claiming your personal power and stepping into your truth, the fullness of your intended identity – this is the joy to be found in your Journey to Wellness. It is a journey to Self and to identifying your chosen way of living now. This is the blessing of one who takes their power to heart.

This is an interesting expression: "taking something to heart." We explore the true meaning of it now. We are to live from our hearts, be guided by our hearts – not our heads – and make heart-centered choices. This path asks us to plant seeds of wisdom within our hearts rather than within our intellects. Investing our selves with trust that our choices are correct is one of those seeds. We have the ability to live forward while thinking forward with a foundation of wisdom and knowledge from our past. This is a great benefit to our continued trust in our selves, trust to be ever guided by our knowingness. Our inner compass.

This surety of direction comes to us with love and guidance from our Higher Self. We are to listen and feel for this guidance during times of need. It will always be our true north star and guide to our best possible outcome.

Balance in life is found when receiving is equal to giving. Consider this and know you will become the teacher as time goes on.

Is Soul Healing About Karma?

You will not be the first to wonder if this is the case.

We assure you that there is a difference between karmic debt, or karmic resolution, and Soul Healing of past life wounds that were received and can be released from connection through this process. There is no reason to think that the Higher Self, your inner wisdom, is anything but eager to help find your path to healing.

There is no need to give in to the feeling, or belief, that suffering through this lifetime is a requirement based on a past life experience, where you may have been victim or victimizer, and a feeling remains that you are not deserving of wellness and joy in your present life. Each person is deserving of health, wellness, and a happy life.

Either way, healing of old wounds and moving into wellness now, with the ability to be healthy and contribute to your world, is the intention we put forward. To do otherwise, to remain in the cocoon when you could become the butterfly and fly free, that would be counterproductive to enjoying a life of wellness, personal strength, and contributing love and healing to others.

It is for this reason that we share Spirit Wisdom on the importance of becoming whole, becoming emotionally and physically healthy, and reclaiming personal power. In so doing, it is clear that awareness returns along with clarity to see options.

If you believe you are to be punished in this lifetime for past transgressions, there is an alternative in thinking and being available to you. Spirit tells us that lessons can be learned in many ways other than living in acceptance of whatever will come in the way of perceived and deserved atonement.

To not enjoy the personal ability to grow and flourish in all ways within all life has to offer is to diminish the gift of this lifetime. Becoming fulfilled and happy is an obligation to self and Self. It is yours to claim. Lifting up the self to achieve and give back to others in teaching, in joy, and in love, these are life rewards to be experienced.

Choose the high road to wellness and bring light to your world. Or, choose the low road and accept what has been and what will be done to you. It is your choice. You have the power to rise and know each lifetime is a new beginning, a blank canvas on which you can paint the story of your life as you intend it to be. Imagine!

Will You Share Your Light with the World?

Personal Power for Earth Healing

In taking back your personal power and recognizing your strengths and abilities, the healing gift to your present self is almost complete. What is left to do, and what will become clear as time goes on, is to create intention for contributing to your greater world and sharing your light. Your inner wisdom and knowingness make you an instrument of healing in your world, whether it be healing of personal wellness or healing of planetary wellness. You have the choice.

For each person gifted with inner knowingness received through this Soul Healing process, there is a piece of Self and ray of wisdom needing to be shared. Where can you make a positive difference? Divinely guided you are to see the way, and so now it is your turn to teach.

A Gift Received Is a Gift to Be Given – Personal Power for Earth Healing

Those with newfound wellness and renewed personal power may look around their selves for a cause to support and contribute to, so that their voices are heard, and impacts felt. Would this pull toward leading be based on what has been reality for them in past lifetimes of influence on your planet or others?

It is what the world needs now: your world and her people, animals, air, water, soil, all resources and living things. Only through living in love will there be care taken to repair and preserve the wellness of your Planet Mother Earth.

This may seem simplistic. You may well ask, "what is my role in this?" Each person who walks your planet has responsibility to tread lightly. Considering the ongoing wellness of both flora and fauna requires deeper thinking about humanity's current actions.

We speak of the taking of resources without concern about their sustainability. We also speak of the increasing awareness of your people that environmental crisis demands attention. This is but one area of life on Planet Earth that benefits now from the reclaimed power of your people. Being willing to take up a cause for wellness on your planet is an extension of your cause to grow into wellness within your self. One benefits the other.

Perhaps you have found, in the search for your past lifetime personas, that you lived as a First Nations person and feel within you reverence for the land and knowledge of medicinal plants. Here is a study you can begin again, which will be relevant to your present times and widely beneficial. This is but one example of past knowledge being brought forward for today's healing.

Consider that whatever strengths and talents you have in this life were also yours in past lifetimes. Consider also that having these gifts, and they are gifts, in this current life indicates a cosmic intention for you to share them with your world for the greater good.

Whether your talents have been built upon and grown for the purpose of a career or a passion, both have their place in your world. For both there can be an extension of these gifts that have been given to you. A gift is something to be given that offers joy to others, through freely sharing your talent. This is the true meaning of gifting. It may be that through finding wellness in your life and reclaiming personal power, a great gift has come to you. Now, it is time to view your self as one who can impact others through your generosity of time and spirit and sharing wellness in joy.

Balance in life is found when receiving is equal to giving. Consider this. Know you will become the teacher as time goes on.

Remember, you are never alone in your journey of life, but always accompanied by your Higher Self, your inner wisdom and guidance, and your angels: the wind beneath your wings. Trust in this.

Living life with chains attached to what does not serve you, this is not a need. What is and should be your need is removing your self from this influence from past times as well as negative influence from the present day. Living in bliss and harmony is your right, everyone's right. It is our intention to show the way to this healed state for each of you.

Trusting and believing in your self, this is another one of your rights. Too often, these have been taken away from children, as well as adults, so that growing into glowing wellness cannot become a reality. We wish to ensure that, even though this may be the case, you have the internal roadmap to your desired destination, which is your return to empowerment.

Claiming your personal power, or reclaiming it, is our chosen state for you and we intend to provide the tools needed for this Journey to Wellness.

What is it that closes the door for you? What hides the pathway to what you can envision for your self? If it is disbelief in your ability to reach it, or worse, a belief you are not deserving, we wish to dispel those beliefs now and penetrate the mists that cover the way ahead. Opening to receive what is rightfully yours, to welcome your hidden or unrecognized abilities – this opportunity is yours to adopt as a new way of blossoming into your true self. Celebrate your self, always. Your Higher Self does so and celebrates each step taken toward release of chains binding you to what no longer serves.

Going forward in life now, with eyes and hearts open to what comes, and in trust that it will be only that which is for your highest and best good – you feel renewed and reborn. In so many ways, you are. Having shed the skin of past darkness and stepped into the light of your new awareness, you are now the teacher and the torchbearer for others.

We did say you, the student will become the teacher in time. Here is the time: now. Yours is the wisdom to share.

Trust in this.
Go in Peace and Love for your reclaimed Personal Power.

~Carole Serene Borgens and
the Divine Spirit Wisdom Source, Pax

Manufactured by Amazon.ca
Bolton, ON

35568882R00111